CELEBRATION
A Washington Cookbook

KYLE D. FULWILER

LADYSMITH LTD. PUBLISHERS
SAINT LOUIS, MISSOURI

Library of Congress
  Catalog Card Number 88-082048
ISBN 0-9611758-2-6

To order copies of *Celebration: A Washington Cookbook,*
send a check for $31.95 ($29.95 plus $2.00 for postage
and handling), U.S. currency only, to: Ladysmith Ltd.
Publishers. P.O. Box 30045, St. Louis, Mo. 63119.
(Missouri residents add 6% sales tax.)

Editing, introduction: Dick Friedrich, Angela Harris,
  Michael J. Salevouris
Art Direction: Beverly Alden Bishop

Cover Artwork: Eric Wiegardt
Regional Vignettes: Nancy Pryor
Book Design and Production: Wiseman Design
Book Illustrations by Brian Barclay
Food Photography: Joel Levin
Regional Photography: Washington State Tourism Division;
  Michael J. Salevouris
Food Stylist: Charlene Howson
Cartoonist: Robert Gallivan
Typesetting: Creative Graphics Center
Color Separations: Lithocraft
Binding: Nicholstone Book Bindery
Printed by Fleming Printing Company
  St. Louis, Missouri

5   4   3   2   1

$29.95

Printed in U.S.A.

To Lela and Cliff Fulwiler

TABLE OF CONTENTS

A LETTER FROM THE GOVERNOR

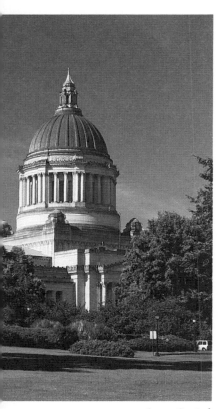

State Capitol

Dear Readers

Thanks to Kyle, I can set the record straight. My preference for hamburgers is greatly exaggerated. Along with guests from around the world who have enjoyed Kyle's culinary artistry at the Executive Mansion, Mrs. Gardner and I are pleased to recommend her newest contribution to Northwest Cuisine.

Many of the recipes Kyle is sharing with you in "Celebration, A Washington Cookbook" have been tested at the Gardner family table and the favorites of family and guests are included here. Our special favorites are Duck with Rhubarb and Cranberry Chutney, Three-Mushroom Soup and Seafood Fettuccine. But all get an A-Plus, and many requests for seconds.

With northwest food and wines gaining fame for the satisfying diversity we Washingtonians have always appreciated, Kyle's performance at the Mansion is a tribute to the fine chefs of the Northwest. Her cookbook deserves a place of honor in any pantry where the abundance of our region is savored.

Booth Gardner
Governor, State of Washington

INTRODUCTION

Growing up in Bellevue, Washington, I was always interested in cooking. I can remember distinctly telling my dad when I was fourteen years old that "When I grow up, I want to go to cooking school in New York." Well, it wasn't New York but London, where I attended the Cordon Bleu School of Cookery. After receiving my certificate in 1977, I returned home to live on Hood Canal, and started my catering business, Cuisine Unlimited. I spent a year and a half as luncheon chef at La Petite Maison in Olympia, then started work at the Executive Mansion during the administration of John Spellman, and stayed on after Booth Gardner's election.

Over the years, I have developed some pet techniques for both preparation and presentation of food, many based on my training at Cordon Bleu, and some growing out of everyday, practical experience. Throughout *Celebration* you will notice that I recommend serving entrees on heated plates or serving dishes. I believe that this is imperative. Think about one poor fried egg going onto a plate that's straight from the cupboard. Through conduction, the egg's heat is lost to the plate, and the egg doesn't have a chance of staying hot.

For a dinner party, you might want to remember to spread the plates out in the oven to heat them quickly. If they're stacked, the outside plates will heat up too much and the inside plates will remain cool. It's little extras like this that, to my mind, make the difference between a good meal and a special one.

I also have some strong opinions on the question of steaming vegetables versus boiling them. At the Cordon Bleu, we were taught to cook flower vegetables in lots of boiling water and to cover root vegetables with cold water and then bring them to a boil—with the exception of new potatoes which should be placed into boiling water. I have firmly adopted the procedure in my own cooking techniques. Many people dispute this method on the grounds that steaming retains more nutrients. I would rather cook broccoli in rapidly boiling water for five minutes than steam it for ten.

Good food, well-prepared, should be available to anyone interested in spending a little time in the kitchen. But the key word in my cooking is "simplicity." Recipes don't have to be complicated or made up of exotic ingredients that require a dozen trips to a dozen different markets. As you'll notice in this cookbook, I enjoy working with traditional dishes and adapting them to the special products we're so proud of here in Washington. You don't have to cook things out of season: use what's available where you are.

And try some of the great Washington wines that are being produced throughout the State as accompaniments to your meals. I've included my own recommendations at the end of each section in the book, but serve your own favorites, too. The reason, after all, to take time and trouble in the planning, preparation, and presentation of a meal is the enjoyment of the meal.

I realized just the other day that I had barely finished perfecting the recipes for this book and was already starting to write new ones. Perhaps that's the element of cooking that I enjoy most: the creativity; I hope that those of you who use this book feel the same way. Personalize your recipes, personalize your cooking, and keep experimenting. You never reach the end.

Although I'm moving to another book, I must recognize the contributions of people and groups whose help, encouragement and patience have seen me through the preparation of this current book. So to Jean Gardner, Booth Gardner, Michi Delaney, Hai Vo, Linda Burgess, Velva Miller, the Governor's Mansion Foundation, the Washington Wine Institute, Ruthann Panowicz of Drees, Olympia, Washington, and to David Galle, I say simply, thank you.

Kyle Fulwiler
Hoodsport, 1988

Eric Wiegardt, Pike Place

A NOTE FROM LADYSMITH

In 1989, the State of Washington celebrates its centennial: one hundred years of statehood. It celebrates, also, its unique Northwest spirit: independence, beauty, unassuming confidence, strength, abundance, wildness, grandeur, directness.

In *Celebration: A Washington Cookbook*, we at Ladysmith not only celebrate the flavors of Washington cooking but the "flavor" of the State itself. From Kyle Fulwiler's artistry in cooking food to Charlene Howson's unerring ability to style it for the camera; from Eric Wiegardt's bold, contemporary watercolor to Nancy Pryor's charming historical vignettes; from the feast of color in Joel Levin's food photographs to the linear simplicity of Bob Gallivan's cartoons, this book is a testament to that unique Northwest spirit that makes Washington State a special place.

It was, in fact, an incident involving several of these people, at the photo session for the food pictures in *Celebration*, that captured for us the essence of that spirit. Charlene had set us the task of sorting strawberries for one of the pictures: our goal, six perfect berries for the Strawberry Blintz photo. After starting with half a flat, we had narrowed down to two dozen berries from which the stylist selected the winning six.

Through the gracious hospitality of the Governor and Mrs. Gardner, and the Governor's Mansion Foundation, we were at work in the Executive Mansion. Nine-thirty in the evening arrived. Everyone was tired and cranky from a long day of painstaking work. The Governor came home from his own long day of painstaking work at the Capitol, and, seeing a tray of perfect strawberries on his kitchen counter, picked one up and popped it into his mouth. In one voice, chef, food stylist, photographer, photographer's assistant, and two editors shrieked "no" at their hard-working governor.

It's an easy assumption that people in power throw their weight around whether they need to or not. Booth Gardner, who might legitimately have yelled back, "This is my kitchen, and what are you still doing here at this time of night anyway," instead apologized, hoping he hadn't ruined something.

That one moment demonstrates some of the characteristics that typify this State and its people: graciousness and informality, unassuming authority, and disarming directness.

Washington cuisine is just one more expression of this complex of qualities. People in the State appreciate what they have. From plains to mountains, from lakes to ocean, from mountain streams to mighty rivers, the gifts of nature abound—a feast for the eye, the spirit, and the palate.

Washington cuisine stresses the fresh fruits and vegetables so abundant from border to border. The fish, the other seafoods, the meats are simply not available in the same way in other parts of the country. Washingtonians have strawberries, blackberries, huckleberries, blueberries, raspberries, peaches, and apples; melons, corn, spinach, herbs, potatoes, and onions; oysters, salmon, clams and crab—all abundant, all fresh.

Kyle Fulwiler, Cordon Bleu trained, brings a special kind of competence to the variety of Washington food. She serves food fit for royalty; indeed on occasion she does serve it to royalty. But it has her signature. Simplicity over elaboration. Fresh foods prepared carefully. Preparations that stress imagination, but start with the qualities of the fresh foods. The star of her show is the food, not the chef.

Like a good umpire in a baseball game, she stays in the background, comfortable with her skills and abilities, knowing that she doesn't need to show off. She knows that the best craftspeople let their work speak for them.

Ladysmith, Ltd., is honored to present the work of this fine chef. You'll find the recipes easy to read, easy to follow, and impossible not to like.

You and your guests will eat the dishes fed to ambassadors and other international figures and share with them the delights of good food well prepared.

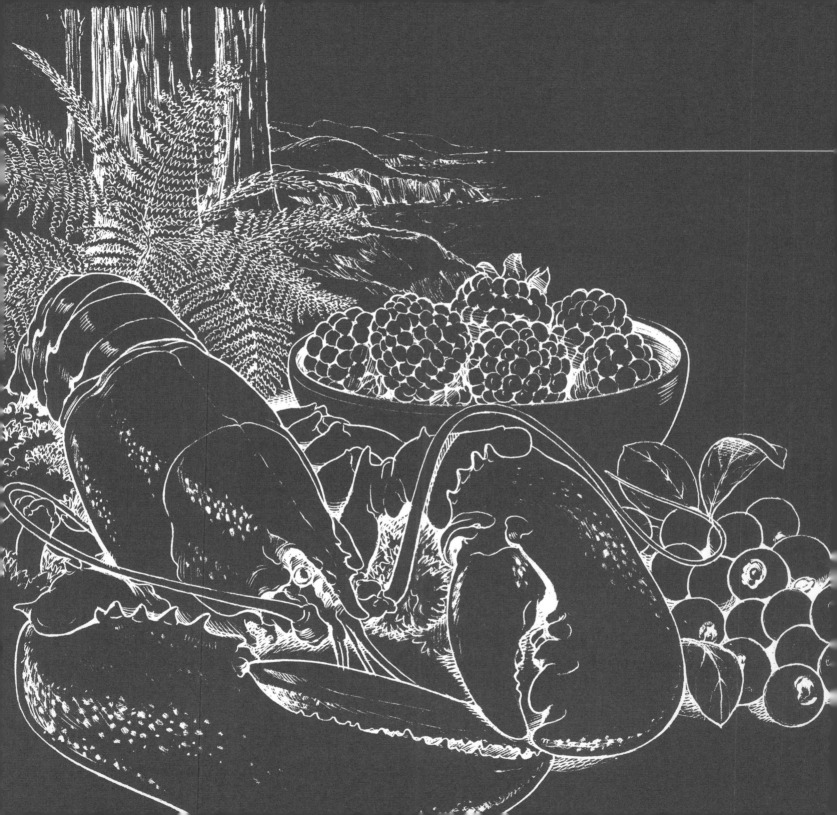

THE COASTAL REGION

During the summer Indian women gathered and prepared vegetable foods, such as roots and berries: including fern, camas and wappato (like our Irish potato) and berries such as salmon, service, huckleberries, wild strawberries, elder, salal, blackcaps and black berries.

SMOKED SALMON SPREAD

1 Pound **Smoked Salmon**
1 medium **Red Onion** chopped fine
1 Tablespoon **Capers** chopped
½ Cup **Mayonnaise**
½ Cup **Sour Cream**
¾ Cup **Celery** chopped
Black Pepper to taste, freshly ground
2 Tablespoons **Parsley** chopped
8 **Lemon Wedges**
1 Baguette **French Bread** sliced into ¼-inch
pieces
½ Cup **Butter**

ASSEMBLY

Flake the salmon into a medium sized bowl. Remove the bones.

Add the onion, capers, mayonnaise, sour cream, celery, and the pepper. Mix them thoroughly.

Line a round-bottomed bowl with plastic wrap. Fill it with the salmon mixture. Cover. Chill for at least 2 hours.

In a medium-sized frying pan, over medium high heat, brown the bread on both sides adding butter as needed. Keep the toasted bread in a warm oven.

TO SERVE: Invert the bowl of salmon. Remove the bowl and the plastic wrap carefully. Garnish the dish with parsley and lemon wedges, surrounded with toast rounds.

SERVES: 10

NOTES & TIPS

One of the nice things about this appetizer is that it works very well as a substantial snack when served with miniature split bagels. You don't need to use expensive smoked salmon so this can be a reasonably priced treat. I recommend it to friends who want to have something to serve on Christmas day for drop in guests: simple yet elegant.

In 1853, Ulysses S. Grant was stationed at Vancouver, Washington. He and three other officers figured that they could make a good profit by growing and selling potatoes, since all foods were quite dear at the time. "Our crop was enormous. Luckily for us the Columbia River rose to a great height from the melting of the snow in the mountains in June, and overflowed and killed most of our crop. This saved digging it up, for everybody on the Pacific coast seemed to have come to the conclusion at the same time that agriculture would be profitable."

HOT CRAB DIP

6 Ounces **Crab Meat**
8 Ounces **Cream Cheese**
1 Tablespoon **Cream or Milk**
2 Teaspoons **Horseradish** or to taste
½ Cup **Almonds** toasted and slivered

ASSEMBLY

Combine the cream cheese with the cream or milk in a medium-sized bowl and mix until they are thoroughly blended.

Stir in the horseradish and crab meat.

Spread the mixture evenly in an 8-inch square baking dish.

Bake at 350° for 25 minutes.

Sprinkle the slivered almonds over the top.

TO SERVE: Serve Hot Crab Dip with crackers or toasted baguette slices. It looks lovely when served in a chafing dish.

SERVES: 8

OVEN TEMP: 350°

NOTES & TIPS

Simplicity is certainly bliss: in five years as chef at the Executive Mansion, I have been asked for this recipe more frequently than I have for any other.

CLAM STUFFED MUSHROOMS

24 **Manila Clams**
24 Large **Mushrooms**
6 Slices **Bacon** *cut into fourths*
½ Cup **Parmesan Cheese** *freshly grated*

ASSEMBLY

Steam the clams until they open. Remove them from the heat. Remove the meat from the shells. Place the clams in a small bowl.

Remove the stems from the mushrooms. Blanch the caps. Drain.

Place them, cap side up, on several layers of paper toweling to remove the excess moisture.

Fry the bacon over medium heat until it is half cooked. Drain the bacon on paper toweling.

Add the Parmesan cheese to the clams. Mix well.

Place one clam inside each mushroom and top each with a piece of bacon. Place them on a cookie sheet. Broil them until the bacon is crisp.

Serve immediately.

YIELD: 24

CRAB BISQUE

¾ Pound **Crab Meat**
3 Tablespoons **Butter**
¼ Cup **Shallots** chopped
2 Cloves **Garlic** minced
2 Tablespoons **Flour**
2 Cups **Chicken Stock**
1 Cup **Whipping Cream**
2 Tablespoons **Cognac**
1 Pinch **White Pepper**
2 **Green Onions** sliced thin

ASSEMBLY

Melt the butter in a medium-sized saucepan over medium high heat until it foams.

Add the shallots, cover the pan, reduce the heat to low. Cook it for about 3 minutes.

Add the garlic. Cook for about 2 minutes.

Add the flour. Stir.

Remove the pan from the heat. Stir in the chicken stock and the whipping cream slowly.

Return the pan to medium high heat. Stir until it boils. Cook for about 3 minutes.

Add the crab, cognac, and white pepper. Bring to a boil. Cook 3 minutes.

TO SERVE: Heat 4 soup bowls. Ladle the soup into the soup bowls. Garnish with the thin slices of green onion.

SERVES: 4

In 1987, Anne Kirske, who was Wine Marketing Program Director here in Washington, asked me to develop some recipes for Washington Wine Month, sponsored by the Washington State Department of Agriculture and the Washington State Liquor Control Board. The idea for this crab bisque grew out of that request and out of my taste for Washington's wonderful Dungeness crab.

Crab Bisque is an especially appropriate "accompaniment" to a number of Washington's premium white wines. Of the eight types of wine grapes that constitute the majority of Washington's harvest, six are white wine grapes. For the white wines I recommend with the recipes in this book, see the "Wine Suggestions" at the end of each regional section.

Mount St. Helens was named for the Irish diplomat Alleyne Fitzherbert, Baron St. Helens.

CRAB CIOPPINO

2 **Dungeness Crabs** *cleaned, cracked*
2 *Tablespoons* **Salad Oil**
1 *Medium* **Onion** *chopped fine*
2 *Cloves* **Garlic** *chopped fine*
4 *Cups* **Tomato Juice**
⅛ *Teaspoon* **Cayenne Pepper**
¼ *Teaspoon* **Red Pepper Flakes**
½ *Teaspoon* **Hot Chili Powder** *or to taste*

ASSEMBLY

Heat the salad oil in a 6 quart or larger saucepan over medium high heat.

Add the onion and garlic. Reduce the heat to low. Cover the pan. Heat for 10 minutes.

Add the tomato juice, cayenne pepper, red pepper flakes, hot chili powder. Increase the heat to high. Bring it to a boil.

Add the crab, reduce the heat, and cover the pan. Simmer for 15 minutes. Adjust the seasonings to taste.

TO SERVE: Heat 4 soup bowls. Ladle the cioppino into the bowls and serve with a hard-crusted Italian bread.

SERVES: 4

NOTES & TIPS

To clean live crab, place crab on its back and pierce the middle of the belly with the point

Crab Cioppino

of a knife This will kill the crab quickly. Remove the back and clean out the insides under cold running water. Now it is ready to be broken into pieces and cracked.

If you prefer to clean the crab after cooking, boil whole for 15 minutes and cool under cold running water, remove back and clean out the insides under running water. When using cooked crab in this recipe, cook the sauce for 10 minutes before adding the crab. Then heat long enough to heat the crab pieces through.

AVOCADO PRAWN SALAD WITH PISTACHIOS

24 **Medium Prawns** *cooked, peeled, deveined*
4 **Avocados**
½ Cup **Pistachios** *shelled, chopped*
½ Cup **Salad Oil**
½ Cup **White Wine Vinegar**
8 cloves **Garlic** *minced*
8 **Lettuce Leaves**

ASSEMBLY

Combine the salad oil, white wine vinegar, and garlic in a medium bowl. Mix well.

Slice 8 prawns lengthwise. Cover and refrigerate them until they're needed. Cut the remaining prawns into ½-inch pieces. Add these to the dressing mixture.

Cut each avocado in half, lengthwise. Remove the pits. Score the inside of each avocado lengthwise and crosswise, and gently loosen the flesh from shell with a spoon.

Cover and set the skin shells aside.

Add the avocado flesh to the bowl with the prawn and dressing mixture. Cover it until serving time. (Stir the salad mixture once or twice while it is chilling if you are not going to use it right away.)

TO SERVE: Chill 8 salad plates. Line them with the lettuce leaves and set one avocado shell on each. Using a slotted spoon distribute avocado-prawn mixture evenly into each avocado shell. Sprinkle chopped pistachios over the tops. Garnish each plate with the reserved split prawns.

SERVES: 8

NOTES & TIPS

An easy way to remove the pit from an avocado is to whack the blade of a heavy chef's knife into the pit, then turn the blade enough to loosen the pit. The pit should lift out easily on the blade of the knife

Some additional garnishes for this salad would be a lemon wheel and parsley along side the small end of the avocado. To make a lemon wheel, cut lemon into ¼ inch slices and then make a cut from the middle through the outside skin, twist it and make it sit upright; stick a piece of parsley on each side.

The town of Artic is not a misspelling of arctic, though many folks think so. It was named for post-mistress Arta Saunders.

THREE-MUSHROOM SOUP

*1 Pound **Shitake Mushrooms***
*½ Pound **Button Mushrooms***
*1 Pound **Oyster Mushrooms** sliced thin*
*4 Ounces **Butter***
*2 Medium **Onions** chopped fine*
*1 Cup **Flour***
*3 Quarts **Chicken Broth***
*½ Teaspoon **Salt***
*2 Teaspoons **Freshly Ground Pepper** or to taste*
*2 Cups **Cream***

ASSEMBLY

Reserve a few of the most attractive mushroom slices for the garnish.

Melt the butter in a large stockpot over medium high heat. Add the onions. Stir them well. Cover the pan and reduce the heat to low. Sweat onions for 10 minutes until they're very soft.

Add the mushrooms. Stir them well.

Add the flour and stir the mixture until the onions are evenly coated. Remove the pan from the heat.

Slowly stir in the chicken broth. Return the pan to medium heat. Stir it frequently until the soup boils.

Season it with salt and pepper. Continue to cook.

Stir until the soup thickens.

Add the cream. Cook just until the soup is heated.

TO SERVE: Heat soup bowls and ladle the soup into them. Garnish with the reserved mushroom slices.

SERVES: 8 16 oz. servings

NOTES & TIPS

I came up with this recipe back when Shitake and Oyster mushrooms still seemed a bit exotic. I was getting excited about these mushrooms and their distinctive flavors and since everyone liked my regular soup, I decided to try a soup featuring them. I remember serving this the first or second time that I made it to the Seattle Consular Corps which is comprised of all the heads of all the different consulates in Seattle. I was really pleased when it went over well with such an interesting mix of people.

Captain James Purrington of Shoalwater Bay "once tried to bake a skunk, but, not having properly cleaned it, it smelled so unsavory with the bake-kettle open that he was forced to throw skunk and kettle into the river, which he did with a sigh, remarking what a pity it was that it smelled so strong, when it was baked so nice and brown."

CRAB CAKES

1 Pound **Crab Meat**
¼ Cup **Mayonnaise**
1 Teaspoon **Chopped Parsley**
1 Stalk **Celery** chopped fine
3 **Shallots** chopped fine
¼ Teaspoon **Tabasco**
½ Cup **Dried Bread Crumbs**
2 **Eggs** beaten slightly
2 Cups **Panko**
½ Cup **Pommery Mustard**
3 Tablespoons **Mayonnaise**
½ Cup **Butter** clarified

ASSEMBLY

Flake the crab meat apart in a large bowl
with two forks.

Add the mayonnaise, parsley, celery, shallot,
and Tabasco. Stir with a spatula until all
the ingredients are evenly mixed.

Mix in the dried bread crumbs. Mix well.

Mix the eggs into mixture.

Place the Panko in a pie plate or other flat,
low-sided dish. Scoop out heaping tablespoons
of the crab mixture onto the Panko, forming
cakes that are 2 inches in diameter and about
⅜ inch thick. Flip each to coat the other side.

Place them on a baking sheet. Chill the cakes
for 30 minutes.

Mix the mustard and mayonnaise in a serving
dish or into individual condiment cups. Cover
and chill.

Heat 2 Tablespoons of the clarified butter in a large frying pan. Fry the cakes, a few at a time, over medium heat, adding the clarified butter as it's needed. Keep the finished cakes warm in a 200° oven.

TO SERVE: Heat serving plates. Set cakes on the plates of a serving platter with the condiment to the side.

SERVES: 20 cakes

OVEN TEMP: 200°

NOTES & TIPS

Panko is Japanese dehydrated bread crumbs, available in many large supermarkets and in Asian markets.

Clarified butter is the oil of separated butter. To separate, melt the butter, skim off the fat and pour off the oil.

RED SNAPPER IN PARCHMENT

8 6-Ounce **Red Snapper Fillets**
6 Cloves **Garlic** peeled
1 Tablespoon **Parsley** chopped
4 Ounces **Butter**
1 **Carrot** cut into matchstick sized pieces
½ **Onion** diced fine
1 Ounce **Butter**
2 Cups **Mushrooms** sliced thin
8 Sheets **Parchment Paper** 12 x 15 inches

ASSEMBLY

Process the garlic in a food processor until it's chopped fine. Add the parsley and process again.

Add the butter and process until the mixture is smooth. Remove it from machine and set it aside.

Mix the carrot with the onion.

Melt the butter in a small saute pan. Saute the carrots and onions over low heat until they're soft. Set the mixture aside to cool.

Place 1 snapper fillet on the bottom third of a verticle sheet of parchment paper. Place 1 tablespoon of the carrot onion mixture on top.

Dot with herb butter. Place ¼ cup of the mushrooms on top.

Bring the bottom of the paper up to cover the snapper.

Fold the sides in like wrapping a package. Roll the snapper over until it's completely rolled up in the paper.

Repeat with the remaining fillets.

Place them on a baking sheet.

Bake in a 400° oven for 15 minutes.

TO SERVE: Place each package on a heated plate. Slit open the tops and peel back the paper.

SERVES: 8

OVEN TEMP: 400°

Red Snapper in Parchment

Captain James Purrington, according to his cabin-mate, "was famous for cooking everything that had ever lived. We had eaten of young eagles, hawks, owls, lynx, beaver, seal, otter, gulls, pelican, and finally wound up with crow; and the crow was the worst of the lot."

SOLE MEUNIERE A L'ORANGE

16 Small **Sole Fillets**
4 Medium **Oranges** peeled
1 Teaspoon **Salt**
2 Teaspoons **Ground Pepper**
1½ Cups **Flour**
1 Cup **Butter**
6 **Eggs** slightly beaten
3 Tablespoons **Parsley** chopped fine
Juice of Two Lemons
Lemon Wheels as needed
Parsley Sprigs as needed

ASSEMBLY

Slice each orange into 8 slices. Arrange them in a shallow baking dish. Keep it in a low oven while cooking the fish.

Mix the salt, pepper, and flour on a pie plate or shallow dish.

Melt 2 tablespoons of butter in a medium-sized frying pan over high heat until it foams.

Dip fillets, two at a time, in flour to coat and then in egg mixture. Cook them quickly on both sides. Keep them warm on a baking sheet in the low oven.

Cook remaining fillets, two at a time. Add more butter as you need it.

Wipe out the pan with paper towels and melt the remaining butter until it's foamy.

Add the parsley and lemon juice. Turn off the heat.

TO SERVE: Heat 8 plates. Arrange 8 of the fillets on the plates and top them with 4 orange slices each. Top each serving with another sole fillet. Reheat the sauce and distribute it over the sole. Garnish with lemon wedges or wheels and additional parsley.

SERVES: 8

OVEN TEMP: 200°

NOTES & TIPS

In my second week at Cordon Bleu in London, we prepared sole meuniere a l'orange and I liked it because of it's simplicity. It wasn't until some years later, however, when lunching at a Seattle restaurant that I was struck by really how good a dish it could be. The next day I started playing around with the recipe until I had a version that suited my taste.

This dish makes an easy, quick, and impressive main course if you wish to have a small dinner party some evening after work. I like serving it with new potatoes and dilled zucchini. Pick up a carton of nice sherbet on the way home for dessert and you have a lovely meal.

DUNGENESS CRAB SOUFFLE

¾ Cup **Dungeness Crab Meat**
¼ Cup **Bread Crumbs** dried
3 Tablespoons **Butter**
3 Tablespoons **Flour**
¾ Cup **Milk**
A dash **White Pepper**
A dash **Tabasco Sauce**
2 **Egg Yolks**
3 **Egg Whites**
½ Cup **Cheddar Cheese** grated

ASSEMBLY

To prepare the souffle, use one of the two following techniques:

1. Wrap a parchment collar extending 3 inches above the edge of a 1-quart souffle dish. Tie it with string.

   Grease thoroughly the inside of the dish and collar. Coat it with bread crumbs.

2. Grease thoroughly the inside of a 1¾ quart straight-sided baking dish. Coat it with bread crumbs.

Melt the butter over medium heat. Add the flour, cook, and stir for 3 minutes.

Remove the pan from the heat. Stir in the milk slowly. Season it with pepper and Tabasco.

Return it to medium heat. Stir to boiling. Boil for 3 minutes, stirring from bottom.

Remove the pan from the heat. Allow it to cool slightly.

Stir in the egg yolks. Blend in the crab and cheese.

Whip the egg whites until they are stiff but not dry.

Fold the egg whites into the crab mixture carefully until the mixture looks streaky.

Pour it into the baking dish. Bake it for 30 minutes at 375°.

SERVES: 4

OVEN TEMP: 375°

John R. Jackson, a bachelor Englishman and subsequently an American citizen, was one of the first settlers north of the Columbia River and Washington's first hotel keeper. Jackson's cabin, erected in 1845 on Cowlitz Prairie, became a convenient lodging spot for travellers. One of the earliest polling places in the area, it later served as a courtroom when Jackson was chosen justice of the peace in 1847. John R. Jackson's cabin started providing good food as well as lodging after his marriage to the widow Matilda Koontz.

LIME BAKED SALMON FILLETS

*8 **Salmon Fillets** 6 ounces with the skin removed*
*2 **Limes***
*4 **Egg Yolks***
*1 Pinch **Salt***
*1 Pinch **White Pepper***
*½ Cup **Salad Oil***

ASSEMBLY

Remove all of the zest from the limes using either a zester or a small grater. Chop the peel fine. Set it aside.

Juice the limes. Strain the juice. Set it aside.

Process the egg yolks together with salt and white pepper until they are mixed thoroughly.

While the machine is running, add the oil slowly.

Add the lime juice and zest. Process until they're mixed in.

Place all of the salmon fillets on a baking sheet. Coat each with the lime mixture.

Bake at 425° for 15 minutes.

SERVES: 8

OVEN TEMP: 425°

Those of us who live in Washington can sometimes become spoiled by the bounty available to us. I admit that it's happened to me now and again. Several years ago, I just got tired of every way I had cooked salmon. My Aunt Hope and Uncle Syl Fulwiler were coming to visit from Spokane and I decided to give this Northwest fish one more chance in their honor. I suppose that most good recipes result from educated taste and the luck of the moment. This one worked so the next morning I got up and scribbled down notes on what I had done. Since then I've perfected the recipe—and recovered from my temporary boredom with salmon.

SALMON WITH MUSTARD DILL SAUCE

8 6-Ounce **Salmon Fillets**
1 Pint **Cream**
2 Tablespoons **Grainy Mustard**
2 Teaspoons **Dried Dill**

ASSEMBLY

Cover salmon with warm water (not hot) in a shallow oven-proof dish. Cover.

Poach in a 350° oven for 20 minutes.

While the salmon cooks, heat the cream in a 10-inch frying pan over high heat until it boils. Lower the heat to medium. Cook, stirring, until it's reduced by half.

Add the mustard and dill. Reduce the sauce until it's thick enough to coat the back of a spoon.

Remove the salmon from the poaching water. Drain it briefly on paper toweling.

TO SERVE: Place each on a heated dinner plate. Top each salmon fillet with about a tablespoon of sauce. Garnish with a sprig of baby dill, lemon wheels, or lemon wedges.

SERVES: 8

OVEN TEMP: 350°

Salmon with Mustard Dill Sauce

New York author Charles Nordhoff observed the Columbia River salmon bonanza in the late nineteenth century. "In this year, 1873, more than two millions of pound were put up in tin cans on the Lower Columbia alone, besides fifteen or twenty thousand barrels of salted salmon."

OYSTERS AIOLI

1½ Dozen **Pacific Oysters** in the shell
2 **Egg Yolks**
1 Teaspoon **Dry Mustard**
2 Teaspoons **Garlic** pureed
1 Tablespoon **Lemon Juice**
1 Cup **Olive Oil**
1 Tablespoon **Hot Water**
Rock Salt optional
¼ Cup **Asiago Cheese** grated
¼ Cup **Parmesan Cheese** grated

ASSEMBLY

Mix well in a food processor or blender: the egg yolks, dry mustard, garlic, and the lemon juice. Add the oil ½ teaspoon at a time with the machine running. Pour the remaining oil in very slowly after the mixture has started to thicken.

Mix in the water once the oil has blended in.

Remove the mixture to a bowl. Cover. Refrigerate this aioli until it's needed.

Use one of the two following techniques for opening the oysters. Shuck the oysters as you would for half shells. Or fill a large shallow baking pan half way with rock salt; place the oysters, cup side down on the salt. Place the pan under broiler heat for 2 to 3 minutes until the shells open. Flip the tops off and continue with the recipe.

Set the oysters on a baking sheet or on a bed of rock salt. (If you used the second method above, simply leave them on the rock salt after opening them.)

Combine the reserved aioli with the Asiago and Parmesan cheeses. Distribute this mixture on the tops of the oysters. Broil them on the bottom rack of the oven until the topping is browned, about 5 to 6 minutes.

TO SERVE: Remove them to small serving plates, three per plate for an appetizer.

SERVES: 6

NOTES & TIPS

If you have 4-inch cast iron frying pans, you can prepare them on the salt in the pans, three to a pan and serve them in the pan.

This recipe is an adaptation of one given to me by Lee Ann Bonacker, coordinator of the Washington Aquaculture Council. My sincere thanks to her.

CRAB QUICHE

1 Cup **Crab Meat**
1 9-inch **Unbaked Pie Shell**
1 Tablespoon **Butter**
½ Cup **Green Onions** *sliced*
1 Tablespoon **Sherry**
1 Cup **Grated Swiss Cheese**
3 **Eggs**
1½ Cups **Cream**
1 Dash **Nutmeg**
1 Dash **White Pepper**

ASSEMBLY

Heat the butter in a small frying pan over medium high heat.

Add the green onion and sherry. Cook until the onions are limp. Set aside.

Mix the eggs, cream, nutmeg, white pepper thoroughly.

Place the crab meat in a pie shell. Cover with the Swiss cheese, green onion. Pour the cream mixture over.

Bake at 350° for 45 minutes to 1 hour, until set firm.

TO SERVE: Be sure to allow the quiche to cool slightly before serving.

SERVES: 6

OVEN TEMP: 350°

Salt Creek County Park near Port Angeles

DUCK WITH CRANBERRY RHUBARB CHUTNEY

1 5 Pound **Duck**
3 Cups **Rhubarb** chopped into 1 inch pieces
2 Cups **Cranberries**
1 Teaspoon **Ground Allspice**
1 Teaspoon **Salt**
1 Teaspoon **Sugar**
½ Teaspoon **Ground Pepper**
½ Teaspoon **Cinnamon**
2 Teaspoons **Szechuan Peppercorns**
6 Tablespoons **Honey**
2 Tablespoons **Red Wine Vinegar**
Watercress Sprigs enough for garnish

ASSEMBLY

Remove the neck and liver from the duck. Reserve the liver.

Cover the neck with water in a small saucepan. Simmer covered for 1½ hours. Remove the neck. Reduce the liquid to 1 cup over high heat. Set it aside.

Prick the duck liberally, all over.

Stuff the duck with 1 cup of the rhubarb and ½ cup of the cranberries.

Lay the duck in an oriental steamer or on a rack in a large pot. If you use the former, fill the bottom ½ full of water; if the latter, add 2 inches of water. Steam the duck for 45 minutes, checking water levels. Add water if it's needed.

Mix the allspice, salt, sugar, cinnamon, and Szechuan peppercorns in a small bowl. Mash them together.

Remove the duck to paper toweling to absorb any excess moisture. Rub it with the spice mixture.

Roast the duck on a rack for 20 minutes at 300°. Increase the heat to 450°. Roast it for another 20 minutes.

Combine the remaining rhubarb and cranberries in a stainless steel saucepan with stock. Cook them for 15 minutes at medium heat. When the mixture becomes lumpy, add the honey and vinegar. Stir.

Remove the duck from the oven. Allow it to rest for 15 minutes. Carve.

TO SERVE: Spoon about ¼ cup of chutney onto the center of a heated plate and surround it with slices of the carved duck. Garnish the plate with watercress.

SERVES: 4 to 6

OVEN TEMP: 300° & 450°

Before the spectacular eruption, Mount St. Helens was a perfect cone—an "American Fujiyama"—reflected in the tranquil water of Spirit Lake.

SEAFOOD FETTUCCINE

1½ Pounds **Fettuccine**
¾ Pound **Small Prawns** shelled and deveined
¾ Pound **Bay Scallops**
4 Pounds **Fresh Manila Clams**
½ Cup **Butter** clarified
2½ Pints **Cream**
1 Teaspoon **Garlic** minced
1 Cup **Parmesan Cheese** freshly grated
Freshly Ground Pepper to taste

ASSEMBLY

Cook the fettuccine in a large stock pot full of boiling water for about 8 minutes or until it's just done. Drain and cool it under cold running water.

Heat 2 tablespoons of the clarified butter in a medium saute pan over high heat.

Saute the prawns and scallops in small batches until they're opaque. As they're finished, remove them to a low oven.

Reduce by half 1½ cups of the cream in a large saute pan over medium heat.

Add the fettuccine. Stir it until it boils. Add the remaining cream and the garlic, stirring to prevent it from scorching.

Meanwhile steam the clams in a large covered pan over medium high heat until they open—about 7 minutes.

The sauce on the fettuccine should be reduced and thick by this point.

TO SERVE: Distribute the fettuccine among 12 heated plates. Top with the prawns and scallops. Garnish with steamed clams.

SERVES: 12

NOTES & TIPS

Manila clams are most often sold as steamer clams. This recipe is very easily halved for smaller groups, but keep in mind that the cream will reduce more quickly with less volume.

I prefer to use linguini in this recipe. Cooking time will vary depending on the type of pasta used.

Seafood Fettuccine

SAVORY RASPBERRY SAUCE

4 Pints **Raspberries**
8 **Chicken Necks, Backs**
1 **Carrot**
1 **Onion** halved
5 **Peppercorns**
1 **Bay Leaf**
6 **Parsley Stalks**
¼ Cup **Red Current Jelly**
¼ Cup **Calvados Brandy**
½ Cup **Butter**

ASSEMBLY

Combine the chicken parts, carrot, onion, peppercorns, bay leaf, and the parsley stalks in a saucepan with at least a 4½ quart capacity.

Fill the pan with water until it's three-fourths full. Bring it to a boil over high heat. Reduce the heat to simmer.

Cook for 4 hours.

Add 3 pints of the raspberries. Continue cooking for 1 hour. Strain the stock and return it to the pan.

Bring it to a boil over high heat. Reduce it by a third.

Add the remaining raspberries and simmer for 15 minutes. Strain the stock again. Return it to pan.

Add the current jelly and calvados brandy.

Bring it to a slow boil over medium heat. Whisk in the butter, one tablespoon at a time

Fish oil was an important condiment for coastal Indians in the Northwest, serving as cream, butter, and salad dressing. The Indians also wore it.

TO SERVE: This sauce is wonderful served over duck or chicken.

YIELD: About 2 to 3 cups.

NOTES & TIPS

You can always have chicken parts on hand if you simply keep them in the freezer as you remove them from any whole chicken you're preparing for other dishes.

The protocol people with the department of trade of the State of Washington told me that duck is regarded as a very honored meat in China, so I developed this sauce to add a Northwest flair to a Chinese tradition and served it to the Vice Premier of China over duck breasts cut on the diagonal.

RASPBERRY MOUSSE

1¼ Cup **Seedless Raspberry Puree**
1 **Lemon** juiced and strained
1 Ounce **Gelatin**
4 **Eggs**
2 **Egg Yolks**
¾ Cup **Sugar**
1¼ Cups **Cream**
2 Tablespoons **Raspberry Liqueur**

ASSEMBLY

Combine the lemon juice in a measuring cup with enough water to total 5 ounces.

Add the lemon-water mixture to gelatin in a small saucepan. Set it aside. (This is called sponging.)

Beat the eggs, egg yolks, and sugar in an electric mixer at high speed until the mixture is very thick and lemon colored.

Mix in the raspberry puree.

Melt the sponged gelatin over medium heat being careful not to scorch it.

Pour the gelatin in a thin stream into the egg mixture while mixer runs at medium speed.

Whip the cream until it forms soft peaks.

Fold it into the egg mixture along with the raspberry liqueur.

Place the bowl over another bowl that contains cold water and ice and stir until the mixture is about ready to thicken.

Pour into 10 individual serving dishes or an attractive serving bowl.

Cover and chill for at least 2 hours.

TO SERVE: Garnish with a rosette of whipped cream and a mint leaf and/or a fresh raspberry on top.

SERVES: 10

Ruby Beach, Olympic National Park

WASHINGTON BLUEBERRY MUFFINS

1 Cup **Blueberries**
1⅓ Cups **Flour**
½ Teaspoon **Baking Soda**
¼ Teaspoon **Salt**
¼ Cup **Butter**
¾ Cup **Sugar**
2 **Eggs**
½ Teaspoon **Vanilla**
¾ Cup **Sour Cream**

ASSEMBLY

Sift together the flour, baking soda, and salt. Set the mixture aside.

Beat the butter and sugar in a medium bowl until they're light and fluffy.

Beat in the eggs one at a time.

Add the vanilla.

Alternately fold in the reserved flour mixture and sour cream.

Fold in the blueberries.

Distribute the mixture into a greased muffin tin. Bake at 450° for 15 minutes.

YIELD: 1 dozen.

OVEN TEMP: 450°

When I attended high school in Bellevue, I had a friend, Renee Rockey, whose parents owned a blueberry farm. I've been stuck on blueberries ever since. In a way, I suppose, they inspired my later experimentation with recipes using blueberries. These muffins are my favorite blueberry treat. I like them even better than blueberries and cream because the sour cream in the batter gives them just a little extra "oomph."

Washington is a berry-picker's paradise. Blackberries, huckleberries, and blueberries can be picked from wild bushes. Somehow these muffins seem to taste better if you make them with blueberries you've picked yourself.

The first known landing on Washington soil by a European explorer was in 1775 when Bruno Heceta sent a boat to the mouth of the Hoh River on the Olympic Peninsula. Hostile Indians killed the landing party.

LEMON MOUSSE WITH BLUEBERRIES

2 small or 1 large **Lemon**
1 Cup **Blueberries**
1¼ Ounce package **Gelatin**
¼ Cup **Water**
3 **Eggs** room temperature
¾ Cup **Sugar**
1½ Cups **Cream**
8 **Mint Leaves**

ASSEMBLY

Remove the peel from the lemons by using a zester or fine grater and set the peel aside in a small bowl. Juice the lemons and strain the juice over the reserved lemon zest.

Add the water to the gelatin. Shake it to remove all air pockets. Set it aside.

Beat the eggs at high speed in a mixer while gradually adding the sugar. Continue beating until the mixture is very thick.

Beat in lemon juice and zest.

Heat the gelatin over medium heat until it is completely dissolved. (Be careful it doesn't scorch.)

Turn the mixer to low speed. Add the gelatin in a thin stream.

Lightly beat 1 cup of the cream. Mix it into the mousse mixture with a spatula.

Set the bowl into a larger bowl of ice water. Stir until it's just to the point of thickening.

Fold in the blueberries.

Quickly distribute the mixture into dessert dishes or champagne glasses. Cover.

Chill for at least 2 hours.

TO SERVE: Just before serving, whip the remaining cream until it's stiff. Garnish each mousse with whipped cream rosettes, using a pastry bag with a star tip. Garnish with a mint leaf on each and a couple blueberries.

SERVES: 8

Lemon Mousse with Blueberries

HUCKLEBERRY COFFEE CAKE

2 Cups **Huckleberries**
⅔ Cup **Butter**
1¼ Cups **Sugar**
2 **Eggs**
1½ Teaspoons **Orange peel**
1 Teaspoon **Orange Flavoring**
2 Cups **Flour**
2 Teaspoons **Baking Powder**
1 Teaspoon **Salt**
¾ Cup **Milk**
¼ Cup **Sugar**

ASSEMBLY

Beat together the butter and 1¼ cups sugar until well mixed. Add the eggs one at a time, beating them well after adding each.

Stir in the orange peel and orange flavoring.

Sift together the flour, baking powder, and the salt.

Mix the sifted ingredients and milk alternately into the creamed mixture.

Stir in the orange flavoring and the huckleberries.

Grease and flour a 9 x 13 inch pan. Pour the batter into the pan.

Sprinkle the ¼ cup sugar over the batter.

Bake at 350° for 40 minutes.

SERVES: 8 to 10

OVEN TEMP: 350°

CRANBERRY SORBET

2 Cups **Cranberries**
4 Cups **Water**
1 Cup **Sugar** or to taste
1 Tablespoon **Frozen Orange Juice Concentrate**
1 **Egg White**

ASSEMBLY

Combine the berries and water in a large saucepan. Bring to a boil over high heat.

Reduce the heat; cover the pan tightly. Simmer for 10 to 12 minutes.

Puree the mixture in a food processor or blender. Press it through a strainer into a large bowl.

Stir in the sugar, orange juice concentrate and egg white. Cool.

Pour it into an ice cream freezer. Freeze according to manufacturer's instructions.

When mixture is finished, spoon into plastic container; cover tightly.

Allow to ripen in freezer overnight.

SERVES: 2 quarts

Lebam, Washington, was named by J.W. Goodell for his daughter. Lebam is Mabel spelled backwards.

KIWI SORBET

8 **Kiwi Fruits** *peeled*
1 Cup **Simple Syrup**
1 Cup **Water**
1 **Egg White**
2 Tablespoons **Lemon Juice**

ASSEMBLY

Puree the kiwi in a food processor or mash them well with a fork. Stir the remaining ingredients into the puree in a medium bowl.

Place in an ice cream freezer and freeze according to manufacturer's directions.

YIELDS: 2 Quarts

Long Beach Peninsula

Narcissa Whitman, wife of missionary Marcus Whitman, wrote to her mother in 1836 describing the garden at Fort Vancouver: "What a delightful place it is, what a contrast to the rough barren plains through which we had so recently passed; here we find fruits of every description, apples, grapes, pears, plums, and fig trees in abundance; also cucumbers, melons, beans, peas, beets, cabbage, tomatoes, and every kind of vegetable. Every part is very neat and tastefully arranged with fine walks lined on either side with strawberries..."

CHOOSING THE RIGHT WINE

Most everyone has heard that red wines go with red meat and white wines go with fish and poultry. These are natural pairings of wine and food, dictated by the flavor and texture of each. Taste a hearty beef stew and you will crave an equally hearty red wine. Poach a delicate fillet of white fish and nothing but a light, dry white wine seems appropriate.

Those natural pairings are obvious, and excellent, choices. But there are endless possibilities within and beyond these combinations. The best way to develop preferences? Taste, taste, and taste some more. Let the flavors of the wines tell you what foods will go best with them. Combine that with your own preferences when choosing wines. There are no rules, only a few guidelines:

—Try to serve wines and foods that match each other for sweetness, richness, and tartness. You'll enjoy a light wine more if you serve it with simple, light food.

—When serving a meal of several courses it is best to begin with a light, white wine and either continue with white wines or go on to reds. You palate will only get confused if you drink white wines after drinking reds.

Adapted from *Vinyard to Vintage: The Washington State Wine Guide*. With permission of The Washington Wine Institute.

THE CHEF'S WINE SUGGESTIONS

Avocado Prawn Salad with Pistachios	*Sauvignon Blanc*
Crab Bisque	*Chardonnay*
Crab Cakes	*Sauvignon Blanc*
Crab Cioppino	*Merlot, Cabernet*
Crab Quiche	*Sauvignon Blanc*
Duck with Cranberry Rhubarb Chutney	*Gamay Beaujolais*
Dungeness Crab Souffle	*Chardonnay*
Lime Baked Salmon Fillet	*Pinot Noir, Chardonnay*
Oysters Aioli	*Sauvignon Blanc*
Red Snapper in Parchment	*Semillon*
Salmon with Mustard Dill Sauce	*Chardonnay*
Seafood Fettuccine	*Semillon*
Sole Meuniere a l'Orange	*Chardonnay*
Three Mushroom Soup	*Chenin Blanc*

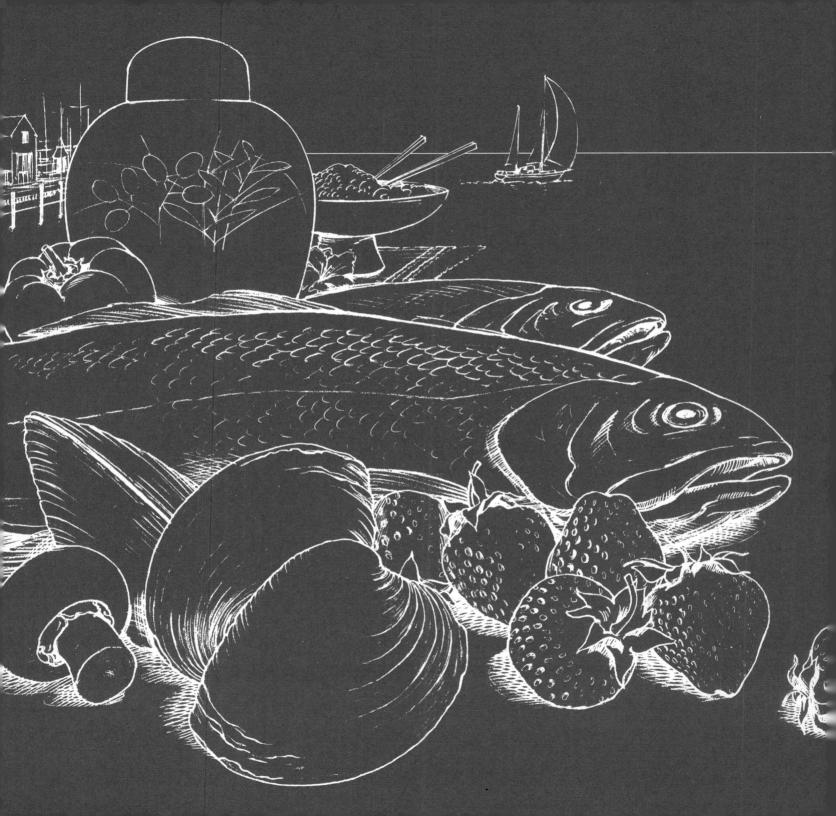

PUGET SOUND

*C*aptain George Vancouver made the first geographical survey of Puget Sound in 1792, naming many geographic features. The Sound itself was named in honor of Peter Puget, one of Vancouver's Lieutenants.

ASIAN SHRIMP &
SCALLOP DUMPLINGS

½ Pound **Shrimp** raw
½ Pound **Scallops** raw
1 6-Ounce Can **Water Chestnuts** roughly chopped
3 **Green Onions** sliced thin
1 Tablespoon **Ginger Root** minced
1 Tablespoon **Sherry**
1 Tablespoon **Cornstarch**
1 Teaspoon **Sugar**
1 **Chinese Sausage** quartered, sliced thin
1 Package (about 40) **Gyoza** or **Sui Mai Wrappers**
Salad Oil for frying
1 Quart **Chicken Broth**
¼ Cup **Light Soy Sauce**
2 Tablespoons **Rice Vinegar**
1 Tablespoon **Sherry**
½ Teaspoon **Garlic** minced
1 Tablespoon **Sugar**

ASSEMBLY

Mince shrimp, scallops, and water chestnuts in a food processor.

Add the green onions, ginger root, 1 tablespoon of sherry, cornstarch, sugar and Chinese sausage. Process until they're well mixed.

Place a level tablespoon of the mixture in the middle of one wrapper and moisten half of the circle edge with water. Fold it in half and seal the edge so it's shaped like a half moon. Fill the remaining wrappers.

Cover them with plastic wrap.

Mix the soy sauce, rice vinegar, sherry, garlic, and the sugar for the dipping sauce.

Heat about 2 teaspoons of oil in a 10-inch non-stick frying pan over medium heat until it's hot. Brown six dumplings on each side. Add ½ cup of the chicken stock. Cover immediately.

Steam them for a couple of minutes. Remove the lid. Let the remaining stock evaporate. Remove them to a platter.

Keep them warm in a low oven while you cook the remaining dumplings by the same method.

TO SERVE: Arrange the dumplings on a serving platter or on individual plates. Serve the dipping sauce on the side.

SERVES: 6 to 10.

NOTES & TIPS

You can make the dumplings in advance. Form them, wrap them in plastic wrap. They can be refrigerated up to six hours before cooking.

The Tacoma Hotel in Tacoma, built in 1888, was designed by Stanford White and completed at the cost of $267,000.

PINECONE CHEESEBALL

1¼ Cup **Whole Natural Almonds**
8 Ounces **Cream Cheese**
¼ Cup **Cooked Chopped Bacon**
4 **Green Onions** sliced thin
¾ Cup **Mayonnaise**

ASSEMBLY

Toast the almonds on a baking sheet in a 350° oven for about 10 minutes. Allow them to cool.

Mix together the remaining ingredients until they're well blended. Shape the mixture into a pinecone shape on a serving plate, fat side down. Cover it and chill for 1 hour.

Insert the almonds into the cone, sharp end pointing out, starting from the bottom, working back and forth, from side to side. Insert them in rows to resemble a pinecone. Place some fir or pine boughs into the bottom of the pinecone for a final touch. Allow it to come to room temperature for about an hour before serving.

TO SERVE: Surround the pinecone with crackers, or serve with a side basket of crackers.

SERVES: 8

Washington State Ferry, Puget Sound

Unmarried women were scarce in the early days of Seattle. Asa Mercer, the University of Washington's first teacher and first president, invited young women of good family to come to the area. Fifty-seven women took up the offer. They may have had second thoughts when they were met by the local men "looking...like grizzlies in store clothes and their hair slicked down like sea otters."

HOOD CANAL
CLAM CHOWDER

2 Cups **Clams** chopped
¼ Pound **Bacon** sliced thin
¼ Cup **Butter**
1 Medium **Onion** chopped fine
4 Stalks **Celery**
½ Cup **Flour**
4 Cups **Half and Half**
4 Cups **Whole Milk**
2 Teaspoons **Salt**
1 Tablespoon **Parsley** chopped fine
2 Teaspoons **Fresh Thyme**
¼ Teaspoon **White Pepper**
3½ Cups **Potatoes** cut into ¼-inch cubes

ASSEMBLY

Fry the bacon in a heavy bottomed 4 to 6 quart saucepan. Remove the pan from the heat when the bacon is just beginning to brown. Drain off the grease.

Add the butter to the pan and melt it over medium heat.

Add the onions. Cook until the onions are soft.

Add the celery. Cook another 5 minutes.

Add the flour. Stir the flour in until it is thoroughly blended. Remove the pan from the heat.

Slowly stir in the half and half and milk.

Return the pan to medium heat. Cook, stirring continually until it boils.

Add the salt, parsley, thyme, and the potatoes.

Cook for about 20 minutes, until the potatoes are soft.

Add the clams. Cook for 10 minutes.

TO SERVE: Heat 8 soup bowls. Ladle the soup into the bowls.

NOTES & TIPS

When I was twenty, I ate clam chowder at a restaurant in Bellevue, and I've been trying to duplicate that taste even since. I think this recipe does it. It is what I think a clam chowder should be—creamy and thick with a good thyme flavor. I hope you agree when you try it.

Anacortes was named for Anna Curtis, wife of Amos Bowman who bought the site and platted the town. The spelling was changed to give it a more Spanish tone to harmonize with the geographic names in the nearby San Juan Islands.

VIETNAMESE STICK BARBECUE

1½ Pounds **Boneless Pork Loin** sliced thin
4 Cloves **Garlic** minced
1 Stalk **Lemon Grass** sliced thin
1 Tablespoon **Sugar**
½ Teaspoon **Salt**
1 Tablespoon **Soy Sauce**
2 **White Onions**
1 Cup **Hoisin Sauce**
1 Teaspoon **Red Pepper Flakes**
10 **Bamboo Skewers** 12 inches

ASSEMBLY

Mix well in a bowl: the pork, garlic, lemon grass, the sugar, salt, the soy sauce. Cover and refrigerate for 2 hours.

Cut the onions into 1-inch pieces.

Place 2 pieces of pork on a skewer, then alternate with a piece of onion until the meat and onion are all used up.

Cook on a barbecue grill or broil until the pork is done, about 15 minutes, turning occasionally.

Mix together the Hoisin sauce and the red pepper flakes.

TO SERVE: Serve the peppered Hoisin sauce as a condiment with the skewered meat.

SERVES: 10

NOTES & TIPS

This recipe is an adaptation of one given to me by Hai Vo, one of the housekeepers at the Executive Mansion.

Washington State has more than 60 premium wineries.

If you prefer, you can use 40 skewers, 5-inches long.

Add fresh or canned pineapple pieces to the skewers for an interesting variation.

Lemon Grass is available in Asian grocery stores.

If you're going to barbecue the pork, soak the skewers for about an hour in cold water to keep them from burning.

SWEET AND SOUR SALAD

2 Tablespoons **Cider Vinegar**
1 Teaspoon **Worcestershire Sauce**
¼ Cup **Sugar**
¼ Cup **Ketchup**
2 Tablespoons **Chopped Onions**
½ Cup **Salad Oil**
1 Bunch **Romaine Lettuce**
½ Cup **Water Chestnuts** sliced
8 Slices **Bacon** cooked and chopped
3 **Eggs** hard cooked, peeled, and chopped

ASSEMBLY

Combine the cider vinegar, Worcestershire sauce, and sugar in a small bowl. Stir until the sugar has dissolved. Add the ketchup, chopped onion, and salad oil. Cover and refrigerate until needed.

Tear the romaine lettuce into bite-sized pieces. Place them in a large salad bowl.

Add the remaining ingredients and toss with dressing.

TO SERVE: Remove the salad from the tossing bowl and place in large glass salad bowl.

SERVES: 8

HONEY MUSTARD SESAME DRESSING

¼ Cup **Sesame Seeds**
½ Cup **Dijon Mustard**
1 Cup **Mayonnaise**
¼ Cup **Honey**
⅓ Cup **Salad Oil**
2 Tablespoons **Hot Water**

ASSEMBLY

Toast the sesame seeds on a baking sheet in a 350° oven for about 10 minutes or until you can hear the seeds popping. Allow them to cool.

Grind the sesame seeds in a blender on high speed or with a mortar and pestle. Set them aside.

Combine the dijon mustard, mayonnaise, and the honey in a medium bowl. Stir them until they're well blended.

Stir in the ground sesame seeds.

Beat in the salad oil slowly a little at a time.

Stir in the hot water slowly a little at a time.

Refrigerate in a covered dish.

YIELD: 2 Cups.

ORANGE BLOSSOM SALAD

2 Oranges
1 Red Onion small
2 Heads Boston Bibb Lettuce
Poppy Seed Dressing (see p. 78)

Poppy Seed Dressing (see p. 78)

ASSEMBLY

Remove the zest from the oranges with a zester or the small side of a grater. Be sure not to remove any of the bitter white part.

Place the zest in a small pan of cold water. Bring it to a boil.

Drain the zest under cold running water. Reserve it until it's needed.

Peel the pith from the oranges with a very sharp knife. Cut them in half lengthwise. Cut the orange halves into thin slices. Cut the slices into quarters. Reserve half of the quarters for garnish and the rest for the salad.

Peel the red onion and slice it into the thinnest possible rings.

Reserve the best rings for garnish and chop the remaining onion roughly.

Tear the lettuce into bite sized pieces. Place them in a large salad bowl. Add the reserved orange quarters and the roughly chopped onion. Toss the salad with the poppy seed dressing, just enough to moisten the salad and not have any remaining in the bowl.

TO SERVE: Chill 8 salad plates. Dish the salad onto them and garnish with orange zest, the onion rings and orange quarters. If you prefer, the salad may be left in the bowl and garnished as one unit.

SERVES: 8

Eastern Washington Forest

Joe Desimone, born in Naples, reigned as the undisputed King of Pike Place Market from 1926 to 1946. He came to the Seattle area in 1897 to work a small rented farm and eventually became the largest stockholder in Pike Place Markets, Inc. He is still remembered at the Market where he is memorialized by the Joe Desimone Bridge, connecting two areas of the market.

POPPY SEED DRESSING

3 Tablespoons **Poppy Seeds**
¾ Cup **Sugar**
1 Teaspoon **Dry Mustard**
½ Cup **Cider Vinegar**
1 Cup **Salad Oil**

ASSEMBLY

Mix on high speed in a blender the sugar, dry mustard, and cider vinegar until the sugar is starting to dissolve.

Change the speed to low. Pour the oil in slowly.

Add the poppy seeds and blend them in well.

YIELD: Makes about 1¾ cups.

NOTES & TIPS

My favorite use for this dressing is in Orange Blossom Salad.

It's also very good over radicchio garnished with blanched julienne strips of orange peel.

Seattle's Space Needle, the towering symbol of the Century 21 Exposition held in 1962, still provides restaurant service and panoramic views of the Sound, the lakes, and the distant mountains.

SEATTLE SUPER SMOKED DUCK SALAD

½ **Smoked Duckling** boned, skinned, julienned
5 Ounces **Walnut Oil**
½ **Red Onion** quartered, sliced thin
5 Ounces **Raspberry Vinegar**
2 Tablespoons **Sugar**
2 Heads **Leaf Lettuce** washed, dried, torn
Black Pepper to taste, freshly ground

ASSEMBLY

Heat 3 tablespoons of the walnut oil in a frying pan until it gets very hot. Saute the duck in the hot oil for 1 minute. Reduce the heat to medium.

Add the onions. Cook until the onions become limp.

Add the vinegar and sugar. Reduce for 1 minute. Add the remaining oil. Cook until it gets hot.

Pour the dressing over lettuce. Toss. Add pepper to taste.

SERVES: 8

SEASHELL PASTA SALAD

8 Ounces **Sea Shell Pasta**
2 **Egg yolks**
A Pinch **White Pepper**
A Pinch **Salt**
⅛ Teaspoon **Dry Mustard**
1¼ Cup **Salad Oil**
2 Cups **Red Wine Vinegar**
3 Stalks **Celery** sliced thin
2 **Tomatoes** peeled, seeded, chopped
3 **Green Onions** sliced thin
½ Pound **Small Salad Shrimp**
2 **Eggs** hard cooked, peeled, chopped
½ **Cucumber** peeled, seeded, chopped
¼ Cup **Chili Sauce**
¼ Cup **Whipping Cream**
1 Tablespoon **Lemon Juice**
A Dash **Worcestershire Sauce**

ASSEMBLY

Liquify the egg yolks, pepper, salt, and mustard in a blender or a food processor.

With the machine running, slowly add ½ of the oil, ½ teaspoon at a time.

Scrape the sides of the bowl.

Mix in the remaining oil and then the vinegar until the mixture is smooth.

Cover and refrigerate.

Cook the pasta. Cool it under cold running water. Strain.

Toss, in a large mixing bowl: the pasta, celery, tomatoes, onions, shrimp, eggs, and cucumber.

Set the bowl aside.

Combine the chili sauce, cream, lemon juice, and Worcestershire sauce with the chilled mayonnaise.

Pour the chili sauce mixture over the pasta. Mix it thoroughly.

TO SERVE: Use this pasta salad either as a first course on lettuce lined plates or else as a side dish for a barbecue.

SERVES: 6 to 8

Seashell Pasta Salad

The first permanent settlers of Seattle named their community New York. As time went by, the new town grew so slowly the settlers added a hyphen and the Indian jargon word "alki," meaning "by and by." The New York part of the name disappeared long ago, but the point on which the settlement began remains Alki Point.

ORIENT EXPRESS SALAD

1 Bunch **Broccoli**
1 English **Cucumber**
1 Cup **Cherry Tomatoes** halved
½ Cup **Rice Vinegar**
2 Tablespoons **Sugar**
1 Teaspoon **Soy Sauce** or to taste
½ Cup Salad **Oil**
1 Tablespoon **Sesame Oil**

ASSEMBLY

Cut the flowerets from the stems of the broccoli and separate them.

Blanch them for 3 minutes. Cool them under running water. Drain them.

Peel the cucumber every half-inch lengthwise to give it a striped effect. Cut it into ¼-inch slices.

Place all of the vegetables in a large serving bowl.

Stir the rice vinegar, sugar, and soy sauce in a small bowl until the sugar is dissolved. Add the salad oil and sesame oil. Mix the dressing ingredients thoroughly.

Pour the dressing over the vegetables. Cover the dish. Marinate it for two hours, stirring occasionally.

SERVES: 8

BASIC VINAIGRETTE

1 Cup **Red Wine Vinegar**
7 Cloves **Garlic** peeled
1 Tablespoon **Dry Mustard**
1 Tablespoon **Black Pepper** coarsely ground
1 Tablespoon **Salt**
3 Cups **Salad Oil**

ASSEMBLY

Mix all the ingredients, except the oil, in a blender at high speed. Reduce the speed to medium when the garlic is chopped fine. Pour the oil in slowly.

YIELD: 1 quart

NOTES & TIPS

The speed at which you pour in the oil determines the thickness of the dressing: the more slowly, the thicker the dressing. The salt may be eliminated.

In 1904 the dinner menu of Seattle's Washington Hotel offered anchovies, a choice of five entrees (including Rissoles of Capon), and a dessert of watermelon Pugette and native grapes. The cost of this feast: 75 cents.

SALAD CHINOISE

½ Cup **Rice Vinegar**
½ Cup **Sugar**
1 Tablespoon Dry **Mustard**
½ Cup **Vegetable Oil**
2 Teaspoons **Sesame Oil**
2 Teaspoons **Toasted Sesame Seeds**
½ Bunch **Spinach**
½ Head **Romaine Lettuce**
½ Head **Iceberg Lettuce**
2 Cups **Vegetable Oil**
1 to 2 Ounces **Rice Sticks**
½ Breast **Smoked Chicken** sliced thin
2 Tablespooons **Toasted Sesame Seeds**

ASSEMBLY

Process in a blender on high speed the rice vinegar and the sugar for about 3 minutes—enough time to dissolve the sugar. Add the dry mustard.

Turn the blender to low speed. Slowly pour in the vegetable oil and sesame oil.

Add the sesame seeds. Set aside until you're ready to toss the salad.

Tear the spinach, romaine lettuce, and iceberg lettuce into bite-sized pieces. Cover. Chill the mixture in a large salad bowl.

Heat the vegetable oil in a deep saute pan over medium high heat. Fry the rice sticks in small batches for about 30 seconds until they're crisp. Drain them on paper toweling.

TO SERVE: Chill 8 salad plates. Toss the smoked chicken with the prepared greens and add the dressing sparingly, just enough to coat the greens, not enough to drain to the bottom of the bowl. Add the rice sticks and toss the salad again. Serve on chilled individual plates garnished with sesame seeds.
SERVES: 8

NOTES & TIPS

Green onion brushes make an attractive garnish and they're quick and easy to make. Simply cut off the root ends and about 5-inches of the green end. Next, make three vertical slices, one inch deep, in the white end. Rotate the onion 90° and make another cut. Repeat, make three more cuts. Now, make 3-inch vertical cuts in the green end and place each onion in ice water for about 1 hour to make brushes. Garnish each portion with a single green onion brush.

In 1876 the St. Louis Hotel in Seattle provided each guest room with a card bearing the warning, "Don't blow out the gas—turn it off, don't whiff it out"—for the benefit of outlanders who were perplexed by the newfangled gas lights.

WALNUT OIL DRESSING

½ Cup **Raspberry Vinegar**
½ Teaspoon **Salt**
2 Teaspoons **Black Pepper** *coarsely ground*
½ Cup **Walnut Oil**
1 Cup **Salad Oil**

ASSEMBLY

Process on high speed in a blender or a food processor for 30 seconds: the vinegar, salt, and pepper. Reduce the speed to medium. Add the oils slowly while processing.

TO SERVE: Use on salads, especially ones using wild greens.

YIELD: 2 Cups

Washingtonians have always enjoyed a good meal. The menu at a January, 1866, party on the Duwamish River included chicken soup, clam chowder, steam clams, smoked, boiled and fried salmon, grouse, ducks, quail, snipe, mashed potatoes, roasted squash, honey-in-comb, wild black-berries, Oregon grape jam, milk and coffee.

MOCHA APPLE BREAD

½ Cup **Espresso** cold
1 Teaspoon **Baking Soda**
1½ Cups **Flour**
½ Teaspoon **Salt**
½ Teaspoon **Ground Cloves**
1 Teaspoon **Cinnamon**
½ Cup **Butter**
1 Cup **Sugar**
2 **Eggs**
½ Ounce **Unsweetened Chocolate** melted
1 Cup **Apple** chopped
½ Cup **Currants**

ASSEMBLY

Mix the espresso and baking soda in a small bowl or measuring cup.

Sift together: the flour, salt, ground cloves, and the cinnamon. Set aside. Beat the butter and sugar together until they're light and fluffy. Mix the eggs in one at a time.

Stir in the melted chocolate.

Alternately beat in the espresso mixture with the flour.

Stir in the chopped apples and the currants.

Pour the mixture into a 9x5-inch greased loaf pan.

Bake the loaf in a 350° oven for 45 minutes.

Cool for 10 minutes. Turn the loaf onto a cooling rack.

YIELD: 1 Loaf

OVEN TEMP: 350°

STRAWBERRY BLINTZES

1½ Pounds **Strawberries** hulled
3 Cups **Flour**
2 Tablespoons **Sugar**
1 Teaspoon **Baking Powder**
1 Teaspoon **Salt**
4 Cups **Milk**
4 **Eggs**
1 Teaspoon **Vanilla**
2 Tablespoons **Butter** melted
2 Tablespoons **Butter**
12 Ounces **Cream Cheese**
1 Tablespoon **Sugar**
½ Teaspoon **Vanilla**
1 Cup **Small Curd Cottage Cheese**
1 Package **Dry Curd Cottage Cheese**
¾ Cups **Sugar**
1½ Cups **Water**
2 Tablespoons **Cornstarch**
3 Tablespoons **Water**
2 Ounces **Butter**

ASSEMBLY

Sift together the flour, sugar, baking powder, and the salt.

Mix well in a blender the milk, eggs, and the vanilla. Add the dry ingredients and mix on low speed until the mixture is smooth.

Add the melted butter. Mix until the butter is thoroughly blended.

Allow the batter to stand at room temperature for 30 minutes.

(continued)

Strawberry Blintzes

Melt about a teaspoon of the remaining butter in a 6-inch frying pan over medium heat. Wipe the pan out with a paper towel.

Ladle 2 tablespoons of batter into the pan. Thin the crepe batter with a little milk if it is too thick.

Swirl the batter around the bottom of the pan, making sure the bottom is completely covered with the batter. Cook until it's set.

Turn the pan upside down to remove the crepe to a baking sheet. (Crepes for blintzes are cooked on one side only.)

Repeat the process until all the batter is gone. (You should end up with about 16 crepes.)

Mix the cream cheese in the large bowl of an electric mixer until it's smooth. Slowly mix in the sugar and vanilla.

Work in the two cottage cheeses until the whole mixture is smooth. Cover. Set it aside.

Puree the strawberries in a food processor or run through a food mill. Add the sugar and mix well.

Heat the pureed mixture in a medium saucepan until it boils.

Mix in a small bowl the cornstarch and the water.

Add the cornstarch mixture to the strawberry puree and cook until it's thick.

Set it aside while assembling the blintzes.

Place the crepes, cooked side up, on a clean work surface.

Distribute the cheese filling in the middle of each.

Fold the bottom side up and over the filling. Fold the sides in and the top down.

Lay the folded blintzes on a baking sheet.

Heat 1 ounce of the butter in a large frying pan over medium high heat until it sizzles.

Brown the blintzes on each side. As they finish, lay each on a baking sheet.

Bake the blintzes at 350° for 10 minutes.

TO SERVE: Either place two blintzes on individual plates and top with strawberry sauce or place all of them on a serving platter and pass the strawberry sauce separately.

SERVES: 8

OVEN TEMP: 350°

STAR FRUIT ICE CREAM

2 Pounds **Star Fruit**
½ Cup **Apple Juice**
2 **Eggs**
1½ Cups **Sugar**
2 Cups **Cream**
¼ Teaspoon **Almond Extract**

ASSEMBLY

Set aside one unblemished star fruit to use sliced as garnish.

Peel the fruit and cut it into quarters lengthwise. Remove any visible seeds (Be sure to look carefully because the seeds are hard to find).

Cut the fruit into small pieces and puree them in a food processor or blender with the apple juice until the mixture is smooth.

Beat the eggs in an electric mixer along with the sugar until they're thick and light yellow.

Stir in the cream and almond extract slowly on low speed.

Add the pureed star fruit and mix it well.

Freeze in an ice cream machine according to the manufacturer's directions.

Slice the reserved star fruit into thin slices for garnish.

YIELD: About 2 quarts.

NOTES & TIPS

This ice cream is "dry" as in "dry" wine. People who are not fond of "sticky" sweet tastes enjoy it immensely.

MACADAMIA NUT PINEAPPLE BREAD

2 Cups **Sugar**
¾ Cups **Butter**
5 **Eggs**
1 Teaspoon **Vanilla**
4 Cups **Flour**
1 Teaspoon **Baking Powder**
½ Teaspoon **Salt**
1 Cup **Macadamia Nuts** chopped
2 Cups **Candied Pineapple**
1½ Cups **Apricot Brandy**

ASSEMBLY

Cream the butter and sugar together until the mixture is light and fluffy. Add the eggs one at a time, mixing well after each. Add the vanilla. Mix thoroughly.

Sift together the flour, baking powder, and salt.

Stir the flour mixture into the creamed mixture.

Fold in the macadamia nuts and candied pineapple.

Grease 2 5x9 inch loaf pans. Line them with parchment paper. Grease again.

Pour the batter into the pans. Bake for 1 hour at 350°.

Remove them from the oven. Cool for 20 minutes.

Remove the loaves from the pans. Place them on cooling racks. Cool them for an hour.

Place each in a glass (or other non-corrosive) baking dish. Pour ½ of the brandy over each. Wrap them in plastic wrap first, then in foil.

Keep them in the refrigerator for at least 2 weeks.

YIELD: 2 loaves

OVEN TEMP: 350°

<hr>

NOTES & TIPS

Loaves of Macadamia Nut Pineapple Bread really make lovely holiday gifts. This recipe doubles to make 4 loaves.

1889 was the year of Seattle's Great Fire. On June 7 a carpenter's glue pot started a blaze which enveloped the entire Seattle downtown area. "Every bank, every wholesale house, every hotel, every newspaper office, and nearly every store was swept out of existence," according to the Seattle Post-Intelligencer.

THE WHITE WINES
OF WASHINGTON

Washington wineries produce primarily white wines. Why? For one thing, the northerly latitude and resulting cooler temperatures make it an ideal white wine grape growing region. Public habits also influence wine production. Since eighty percent of the wines consumed in America are white, logic and desire to please the public dictated that Washington winemakers initially concentrate on white wines. The economics of aging wine has also influenced its production. White wines are often drinkable as soon as the spring after harvest; red wines require longer aging. Rather than keeping working capital tied up in wines that require aging, winemakers often begin by making white wines.

The premium Washington State white wines include Johannisberg and White Riesling, made from the great grape of Germany, Chenin Blanc of the Vouvray region in France, Sauvignon Blanc and Semillon from Bordeaux, and Chardonnay of the Burgundy and Champagne regions. White wines are also made from Gewurztraminer, Muscat, Madeline Angevine and others.

Adapted from *Vinyard to Vintage: The Washington State Wine Guide.* With permission of The Washington Wine Institute.

THE CHEF'S WINE SUGGESTIONS

Floating Island Pudding	*Muscat*
Sweet and Sour Salad	*Gewurztraminer*
Hood Canal Clam Chowder	*Sauvignon Blanc*
Salad Chinoise	*Dry Riesling*
Seattle Super Smoked Duck Salad	*Sauvignon Blanc*
Strawberry Blintzes	*Sparkling Riesling*
Vietnamese Stick Barbecue	*Cabernet*

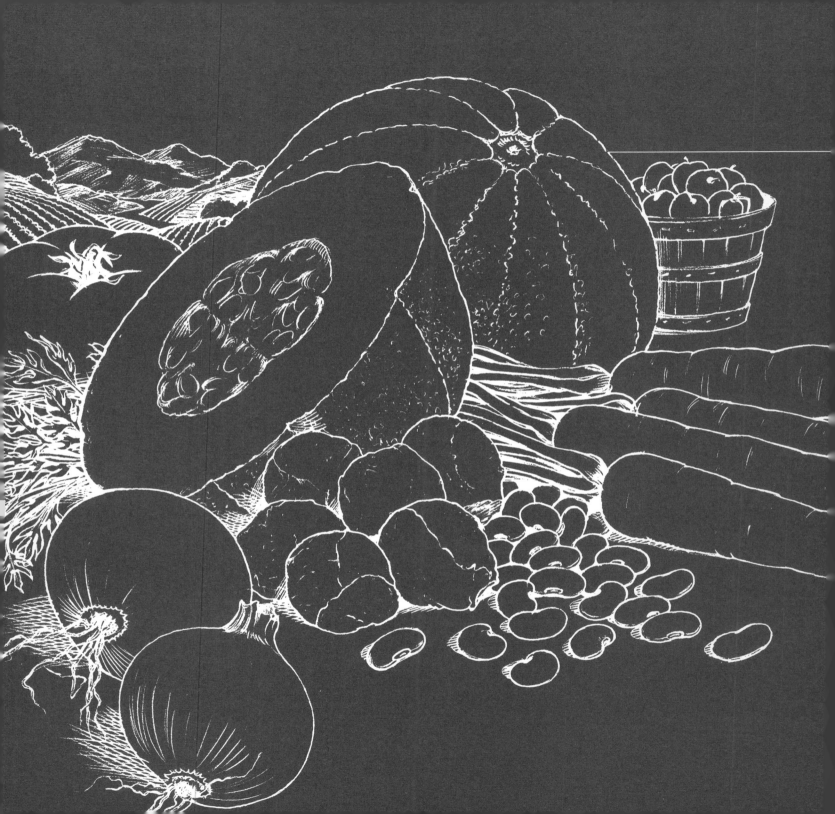

FERTILE VALLEYS

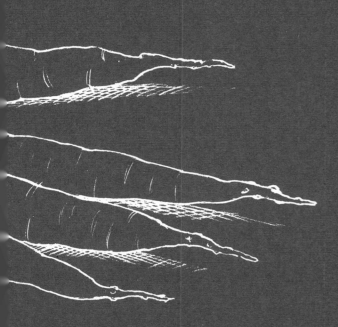

*H*ops, spearmint oil, sweet cherries, apples, carrots, red raspberries, potatoes, pears, apricots, asparagus, green peas: Washington is a leading national producer of these crops.

CHILI AVOCADO DIP

6 **Ripe Avocados**
½ Cup **Chopped Green Chilies**
5 **Green Onions** chopped fine
2 Tablespoons **Fresh Lemon Juice**
¼ Cup **Mayonnaise**
1 Teaspoon **Salt**
6 Drops **Tabasco Sauce**

ASSEMBLY

Peel the avocados, dice them, and mash them in a medium-sized bowl until they're almost smooth.

Add the remaining ingredients and mix them until they're thoroughly blended.

Cover the dip and refrigerate it until serving time.

TO SERVE: Chill the serving bowl you're going to use and fill with the dip. Surround the bowl with tortilla chips.

SERVES: 3 cups

NOTES & TIPS

Chopped, seeded tomato may be added. This dip also makes an excellent filling for omelettes.

Chili Avocado Dip is another of what I call "substantial" snacks. Fry your own corn tortillas into chips to serve with the dip and you won't need anything else. If you're expecting guests at that odd time of day—too late for lunch, too early for dinner, serve this combination. It's tasty and satisfying.

The recipe itself is based on one from my godmother Carolyn Mueller. She had an avocado tree in her backyard in Whittier, California, and after a number of different uses settled on her version of the dip as her favorite avocado use.

Seattle's Pike Place Market was established at the foot of Pike Street in 1907. It was a place where local farmers could sell their produce from horse-drawn wagons. Soon buildings were constructed as a protection from the persistent Seattle rains and the market was on its way to becoming a local institution.

STUFFED
NEW RED POTATOES

50 **New Red Potatoes** *extra small*
24 Ounces **Cream Cheese**
¼ Cup **Mayonnaise**
⅛ Teaspoon **White Pepper**
1 Tablespoon **Dried Dill**
Caviar *as needed, 3 colors if desired*
1 Bunch **Fresh Baby Dill**
Green Leaf Lettuce *as needed*

ASSEMBLY

Cut a small slice from each potato. Cut the ones larger than 1½-inches in half.

Cook the potatoes in a large pot of boiling water, about 12 minutes. Do not overcook.

Drain the potatoes. Allow them to cool.

Combine in an electric mixer or by hand: the cheese, mayonnaise, pepper, and the dried dill. Whip this mixture until it's smooth. Put it into a pastry bag with a ½ inch star tip. Set it aside.

Place the potatoes, cut side down on a tray. Cut a hole out of the top of each using a melon baller.

Pipe a generous amount of the cheese mixture into each potato.

TO SERVE: Garnish the tops with caviar and a sprig of fresh dill. Place them on a tray lined with green leaf lettuce.

SERVES: 25 as an appetizer

Stuffed New Red Potatoes

DEEP FRIED ZUCCHINI WITH CITRUS DIP

6 **Medium Zucchini** *cut into ¼-inch slices*
2 **Egg Yolks**
1 *Teaspoon* **Dry Mustard**
½ *Teaspoon* **Salt**
½ *Teaspoon* **White Pepper**
1¼ *Cup* **Vegetable Oil**
1 *Tablespoon* **White Wine Vinegar**
Peel of one Orange *grated*
½ *Orange's* **Orange Juice**
3 *Cups* **Bread Crumbs** *fresh*
½ *Cup* **Parmesan cheese** *grated*
4 **Eggs**
1 *Teaspoon* **Vegetable Oil**
1 *Teaspoon* **Water**
Oil *for deep frying*

ASSEMBLY

Liquify the egg yolks, dry mustard, salt, and white pepper in a food processor or blender.

Add the oil slowly while processing. Add the vinegar as the mixture thickens.

Add the orange peel and orange juice. Process until it is completely incorporated.

Refrigerate this mixture.

Combine the fresh bread crumbs and Parmesan cheese in a shallow dish or pie pan.

Beat the eggs, vegetable oil, and water.

Heat the oil in a deep fat fryer or heavy saucepan. (If the latter, use about 2 inches of oil.)

Add the sliced zucchini, a few at a time, to the egg mixture. Dip the slices in the crumbs one at a time. Drop them in hot oil.

Remove each when it becomes golden brown. Place them in a pan lined with paper towels. Hold them in a warm oven.

TO SERVE: Place a bowl of the chilled citrus dip in the center of the serving plate, then surround the bowl with zucchini.

SERVES: 6-8

At the turn of the century hundreds of gold-hungry miners swarmed the streets of the placer mining camp of Liberty. Today only their memory lingers as a few weekend prospectors pan for gold in the surrounding creeks.

APPLE CHEDDAR SOUP

6 **Apples** peeled, cored, chopped roughly
¼ Cup **Butter**
1 Tablespoon **Calvados Brandy**
4 Cups **Chicken Stock**
⅛ Teaspoon **Cinnamon**
¼ Teaspoon **Freshly Ground Nutmeg**
⅛ Teaspoon **White Pepper**
1 Cup **Cream**
2 **Egg Yolks**
¼ Teaspoon **Garlic Puree**
1 Cup **Fresh White Bread Crumbs**
½ Cup **Salad Oil**
3 Cups Grated **Sharp Cheddar Cheese**
2 Tablespoons Freshly Grated **Parmesan Cheese**

ASSEMBLY

Melt the butter in a large (six quart or larger) heavy bottomed pan or stockpot, over medium heat. Add the apples and Calvados. Reduce the heat to low and allow the apples to soften for 10 minutes.

Add the chicken stock and allow it to cook until it's soft and pulpy.

Puree the apples in a food processor or blender. Return to the pan or stock pot.

Add the cinnamon, nutmeg, white pepper and cream. Bring it to a boil. Set it aside while making the cheese mixture.

Process the egg yolks with the garlic puree in a food processor until they are thoroughly mixed.

Add the bread crumbs. Dribble in 3 table-spoons of the oil with the machine running. Pour in the rest slowly in a thin stream.

Add the two cheeses and process until smooth.

TO SERVE: Heat 8 bowls. Reheat the soup to boiling and ladle into bowls. Top each with a spoonful of cheese mixture and serve.

SERVES: 8 8 oz. servings

NOTES & TIPS

I came up with this recipe especially for a Governor's Mansion Foundation fundraiser. They wanted to print a menu card and so they needed the menu a long time before the event. I had eaten a bite of fresh apple pie with cheddar cheese melted on it the weekend before. It tasted so good I took the risk of putting it on a menu before I even had a recipe.

CARROT PEANUT SOUP

2 Cups **Carrots** *peeled, sliced thin*
1 Cup **Chunky Peanut Butter**
½ Cup **Butter**
½ Cup **Onions** *chopped*
½ Cup **Celery** *sliced thin*
3 Tablespoons **Flour**
6 Cups **Chicken Stock**
1 Cup **Half and Half**

ASSEMBLY

Melt the butter in a large sauce pan over medium heat until it's foamy. Add the carrots, onions, and celery.

Reduce the heat to medium and cover. Cook until the vegetables are soft but not brown, about 10 minutes.

Remove the pan from the heat and sprinkle flour over the hot mixture. Stir well. Add the chicken stock slowly, stirring constantly.

Return to medium high heat, continuing to stir until boiling. Reduce the heat to simmer; cook for 30 more minutes.

Remove from the heat. Allow it to cool slightly.

Puree the mixture in a food processor or food mill until it's smooth. Place the peanut butter in a large bowl. Stir in the pureed mixture slowly until it's smooth.

Place in pan. Pour in the half and half.

Heat until boiling.

TO SERVE: Heat 6 to 8 bowls. Ladle the soup in just before you're ready to serve.
SERVES: 6 to 8

NOTES & TIPS

I was one of the founding members of the Northwest Culinary Alliance and during the time we were writing the by-laws for the group, we would have marathon meetings to accomplish this task. The person having the meeting would make the lunch. One meeting there was carrot soup and then a few nights later I was eating in a restaurant that served peanut soup as a first course. Then it struck me: making a soup with both the carrot and peanut flavor.

The Washington state flower is the Coast Rhododendron and the state dance is the Square Dance.

GAZPACHO

6 **Tomatoes** *peeled, seeded, chopped*
4 Cups **Tomato Juice**
1 **Cucumber** *peeled, seeded, chopped fine*
1 **Green Pepper** *seeded, chopped fine*
1 **White Onion** *chopped fine*
3 Cloves **Garlic**
½ Teaspoon **Salt**
⅛ Teaspoon **Cayenne Pepper**
⅛ Teaspoon **White Pepper**
½ Teaspoon **Chili Powder** *or to taste*
1 Cup **Sour Cream**

ASSEMBLY

Puree the tomatoes with the juice in a food processor. Pour the mixture into a large bowl.

Add the cucumbers, green peppers, and onion.

Crush the garlic on a flat surface with the side of a table knife.

Sprinkle the salt over the garlic. Continue crushing it until it's smooth. Add it to the tomato mixture.

Add the cayenne, white pepper, and the chili powder.

Stir it until the seasonings are mixed in thoroughly. Cover.

Chill at least 3 hours.

TO SERVE: Chill 8 soup bowls. Ladle the soup into them and garnish with a dollop of sour cream in each bowl.

SERVES: 8

Skagit Valley Tulip Field

CREAM OF BROCCOLI SOUP

12 Stalks **Broccoli** peeled, sliced thin
1 Cup **Broccoli Flowerets** chopped
3 Ounces **Butter**
2 Medium **Onions** chopped fine
6 Cups **Chicken Stock**
2 Cups **Cream**
2 Dashes **White Pepper**
1 Tablespoon **Soy Sauce**

ASSEMBLY

Blanch the broccoli flowerets in boiling water for 1 minute. Drain them in a strainer. Run cool water over them and set aside.

Melt the butter in a 6 quart saucepan until it's foamy. Add the chopped onion, chopped broccoli stalks. Cover. Heat over low heat for 15 minutes.

Add the chicken stock. Simmer for 30 minutes.

Remove it from the heat. Puree the mixture in a blender or a food processor.

Return the puree to a pan. Add cream, white pepper and soy sauce. Bring to a boil, add the chopped flowerets and cook for 3 more minutes.

TO SERVE: Heat 8 soup bowls. Ladle the soup into the bowls and granish with croutons. (See "Tips" below.)

SERVES: 8

For a crouton garnish: cut firm white bread into ¼-inch cubes; fry until golden in ¼-inch salad oil. Drain on paper toweling. Sprinkle over soup just before serving.

I suppose every cook has a favorite recipe. This is mine—just because it's wonderful. Everybody has days when it seems like "this world isn't treating me right." When that happens I treat myself to cream of broccoli soup, a chicken sandwich on toasted white bread, and I sit in my living room to eat, looking out at Hood Canal and the hills to the east. My sure cure for the blues.

"Alki," a Chinook word, meaning "by and by" is the State Motto.

ZILLAH CHILI SOUP

1 28 Ounce Can **Whole Tomatoes**
1 15 Ounce Can **Red Kidney Beans** drained
1 15 Ounce Can **Pinto Beans** drained
6 Cups **Water**
3 Tablespoons **Tomato Paste**
1 Tablespoon **Chili Powder**
¼ Teaspoon **Cayenne**
1 Teaspoon **Salt**
1 Tablespoon **Brown Sugar**
1 Tablespoon **Worcestershire Sauce**
1 Teaspoon **Hot Pepper Flakes**
1 Cup **Beef Stock**
½ Teaspoon **Garlic Puree**
1 Cup **Grated Cheddar Cheese**
1 Bunch **Green Onions** sliced thin
1 Cup **Sour Cream**

ASSEMBLY

Mash the tomatoes in a large saucepan until they're broken up.

Add the kidney beans, pinto beans, and water. Heat over medium high heat.

Stir in the tomato paste until it's incorporated.

Add the chili powder, cayenne, salt, brown sugar, Worcestershire sauce, hot pepper flakes, beef stock and garlic puree.

Continue to heat until it's boiling, then simmer it for 20 minutes.

Place the grated cheese, green onion, sour cream into separate bowls.

Zillah Chili So

TO SERVE: Heat 8 bowls. Ladle the soup into them. Allow the guests to top their own soup with the cheese, onion, sour cream.

SERVES: 8 8 ounce servings

NOTES & TIPS

Wonderful on a cold day; easy to prepare after work.

The town of Zillah got its name from the daughter of T.F. Oakes, president of the Northern Pacific.

SPINACH SOUP

5 Bunches **Spinach**
4 Ounces **Butter**
3 **Medium Onions** chopped fine
5 Tablespoons **Flour**
1½ Quarts **Chicken Stock**
⅛ Teaspoon **Freshly Grated Nutmeg** or to taste
⅛ Teaspoon **White Pepper**
½ Teaspoon **Lemon Juice**
1 Pint **Cream**
4 **Eggs** hard cooked, peeled, chopped

ASSEMBLY

Wash the spinach in several changes of cold water and break off all but 2-inches of the stems.

Blanch it in a very large pot of boiling water for 2 minutes. Drain and cool it quickly under cold running water. Remove as much excess water as possible by squeezing a handful of spinach at a time. Set it aside.

Melt the butter over medium high heat in a 6-quart sauce pan until it's foamy. Add the onions and cover. Reduce the heat to low. Allow them to sweat for 10 minutes.

Remove the pan from the heat. Stir in the flour thoroughly.

Slowly stir in the stock. Return the pan to medium high heat. Stir the liquid until it boils.

Add the spinach and cook for 2 minutes.

Puree the mixture in a food processor or blender and return to the pan.

Add the nutmeg, white pepper, lemon juice and cream. Bring it back to a boil.

TO SERVE: Heat 8 soup bowls. Ladle the soup into the bowls and garnish with generous amounts of chopped hard-cooked egg.

SERVES: 8 12-ounce servings.

NOTES & TIPS

As you have worked your way through this book, you've probably noticed that I make vegetable soups that are mainly pureed vegetables. I like my soups to be substantial and want the rich natural tastes of the main ingredients to stand out. This spinach soup, one of Jean Gardner's favorites, is no exception.

DAVID'S SPINACH SALAD

2 Bunches **Spinach** cleaned, dried, torn into
1-inch pieces
4 **Eggs** hard cooked, peeled, chopped
1 Cup **Monterey Jack Cheese** grated
½ Cup **Bacon Bits**
½ Cup **Sunflower Seeds**
1½ Cup **Mushrooms** sliced thin
1 Cup **Olive Oil**
1 Tablespoon **Lemon Juice**
¼ Cup **Romano Cheese** grated
1 Tablespoon **Dried Oregano**
2 **Eggs**
1-2 **Tomatoes** cut into 16 wedges

ASSEMBLY

Toss in a large salad bowl: the spinach, hard cooked eggs, Monterey Jack cheese, the bacon bits, sunflower seeds, and the mushrooms.

Whisk vigorously: the olive oil, lemon juice, Romano cheese, the dried oregano, and the eggs.

Pour the dressing over the salad. Toss.

TO SERVE: Chill 8 salad plates. Divide the salad among them. Garnish each salad with tomato wedges.

SERVES: 8

Tulip

GINGER CARROTS

8 **Carrots** peeled, halved lengthwise
2 Tablespoons **Fresh Ginger** chopped fine
½ Cup **Chicken Stock**
¼ Cup **Honey**

ASSEMBLY

Set the carrots cut side down on a cutting board. Cut them into ¼-inch slices diagonally.

Add the ginger and chicken stock to the sliced carrots in a frying pan.

Heat over high heat until the liquid has nearly evaporated completely, stirring occasionally.

Stir in the honey watching carefully to prevent scorching. Carrots are done when all the liquid has evaporated.

SERVES: 8

Washington's finest wine grape growing regions share the same northerly latitude as France's Burgundy and Bordeaux regions.

CHATEAU POTATOES

5 Medium to Large **Potatoes** *peeled, quartered lengthwise*
3 Ounces **Butter**

ASSEMBLY

Bevel the edges of the potatoes with a vegetable peeler to make them appear round and oblong, like elongated eggs.

Blanch the potatoes in at least 2 quarts of water for about 10 minutes or until they are tender to the fork. Do not overcook. Check for tenderness after about 6 minutes. Drain.

Melt the butter in a small saucepan. Dip each potato into the butter and coat. Place each on a baking sheet.

Bake for about 15 minutes at 350° or until golden brown.

Turn each potato and bake for another 10 minutes.

SERVES: 8

OVEN TEMP: 350°

NOTES & TIPS

Cooking time for the potatoes will depend on the size and age of the potatoes. You can prepare and blanch the potatoes earlier in the day, then hold them at room temperature until it's time to coat them with butter.

Use leftovers for hash browns.

SCALLOPED POTATOES GRUYERE

6 **Potatoes** peeled and sliced thin
Salt to taste
White Pepper to taste
½ Pound **Gruyere Cheese** grated
¼ Cup **Butter**
½ Cup **Milk**

ASSEMBLY

Place ⅓ of the potatoes in a greased 8-inch square baking dish. Sprinkle this layer with salt, pepper, ⅓ of the cheese, and 1 tablespoon of the butter. Repeat twice, making three layers.

Top them with the remaining butter.

Pour the milk over all.

Bake the dish at 350° for 45 minutes or until the potatoes are tender.

SERVES: 8

OVEN TEMP: 350°

Columbia River Gorge

The St. Charles Winery, on Stretch Island, was Washington's first post-prohibition winery.

MOLDED SPINACH CREAMS

2½ Pounds **Fresh Spinach** *cleaned and clipped*
2 Tablespoons **Butter**
3 Tablespoons **Butter**
3 Tablespoons **Flour**
2 Cups **Milk**
3 **Eggs**
¼ Teaspoon **Salt**
Freshly Ground Pepper *to taste*
Freshly Grated Nutmeg *to taste*

ASSEMBLY

Blanch the spinach in a large pot of boiling water for 3 minutes. Drain and cool under cold running water.

Squeeze out as much water as possible.

Melt the 2 tablespoons of butter in a medium sized frying pan.

Add the spinach. Stir it and cook to drive off any of the excess moisture. Remove the pan from the heat. Set it aside.

Melt the 3 tablespoons of butter in a medium sized saucepan over medium heat.

Add the flour. Cook for about 3 minutes.

Remove the saucepan from the heat. Stir in the milk slowly.

Bring to the mixture to the boil. Let it cook until it's very thick.

Remove it from the heat. Allow it to cool slightly.

Process the spinach and the sauce together in a food processor until they are well mixed.

Add the eggs, salt, pepper, and the nutmeg. Continue to process until the mixture is blended.

Grease 10 dariole molds or oven proof ramekins and distribute the spinach mixture equally among them. Leave about a ½-inch at the top of each mold.

Cover each with a square of foil and place them in a shallow baking dish.

Add enough water to the baking dish so that the level is three-fourths of the way up the sides of the molds.

Bake at 350° for about 25 minutes or until the molds are firm.

TO SERVE: Run a knife gently around the inside of each mold and invert each onto a plate.

SERVES: 10

OVEN TEMP: 350°

NOTES & TIPS

The quantity may vary according to the size of molds you use; this recipe is geared to a 6-ounce mold.

CREAMED SPINACH PARMESAN

3 Bunches **Spinach** *cleaned, stems trimmed*
to 1 inch
4 Tablespoons **Butter**
4 Tablespoons **Flour**
1¼ Cups **Milk**
⅛ Teaspoon **Nutmeg**
1 Dash **White Pepper**
1 Dash **Salt**
2 **Eggs**
¼ Cup **Grated Parmesan Cheese**

ASSEMBLY

Melt ½ of the butter in a medium saucepan. Add the flour. Cook until the flour is golden. Remove from heat.

Slowly stir in the milk until the mixture is smooth. Add the nutmeg, white pepper, salt.

Return the mixture to the heat. Bring it to the boil slowly. Cook for 3 minutes.

Remove it from the heat. Cool it slightly.

Blanch the spinach in boiling water for 3 minutes. Drain it into a colander. Cool it under running water. Drain the spinach until it is as dry as you can get it.

Heat the remaining butter until it's foamy. Add the spinach. Cook until any moisture is gone, about 5 minutes.

Puree the spinach in a food processor or a blender.

Add the sauce, eggs, Parmesan. Process the mixture until it is well mixed.

Bake the spinach mixture in a greased 8-inch square baking dish at 350° for 30 minutes.

SERVES: 4 to 8

OVEN TEMP: 350°

NOTES & TIPS

I served this at a formal dinner once, just as a filler. Surprisingly it was the hit of the meal—spinach, the star of a formal dinner!

Washington has so many trees, it should come as no surprise that petrified wood is the State gem. Ginkgo Petrified Forest State Park near Vantage boasts over 200 species of fossil wood.

LITTLE CREAMY CABBAGES

1 Pound **Brussels Sprouts** trimmed, halved
lengthwise
½ Cup **Chicken Stock**
½ Cup **Sour Cream**
1 Tablespoon **Prepared Horseradish**

ASSEMBLY

Wash the Brussels sprouts thoroughly in cold water. Drain them.

Heat the sprouts and chicken stock in a 12-inch frying pan over medium heat until they boil. Cook for 3 minutes.

Uncover. Allow the liquid to evaporate while watching it carefully.

Add the sour cream and horseradish. Cook until just heated through.

SERVES: 6 to 8.

NOTES & TIPS

When I was a child I thought this vegetable was so cute I begged my mother until she bought some. Of course, after I tasted them I didn't think that they were so cute anymore. Cooked this way, I now believe they're "cute" again. Or have my tastes grown up too?

DILLED ZUCCHINI

*4 Medium **Zucchini** cut into ¼-inch rounds*
*½ Cup **Dry White Wine***
*1 Ounce **Butter** melted*
*1 Teaspoon **Dried Dill***
***Freshly Ground Pepper** to taste*

ASSEMBLY

Cook the zucchini in the wine in a covered saute pan over high heat until it is steaming. Remove the pan from the heat. Drain off the liquid.

Add the melted butter, dill, and pepper.

SERVES: 8

The Klickitat County Historical Museum contains the largest collection of antique coffee grinders in the United States.

MINT SAUCE

½ Cup **Fresh Mint Leaves** loosely packed
3 Tablespoons **Sugar**
3 Tablespoons **Cider Vinegar**

ASSEMBLY

Process the mint and sugar in a food processor until the mint is chopped fine.

Add the vinegar. Process the mixture.

YIELD: ¾ Cup

NOTES & TIPS

This is a sharp tasting mint sauce especially good when used as an accompaniment to roasted lamb or broiled lamb chops. It's a nice alternative to the dreary mint jelly so often served with lamb.

The town of Ellensburg gained a measure of respectability when it was renamed for Mary Ellen Shoudy, wife of the man who platted the city. It had originally been called Robbers Roost.

CANTALOUPE SHERBET

8 Cups **Pureed Cantaloupe**
6 **Egg Whites**
½ Teaspoon **Cream of Tartar**
2½ Cups **Sugar**
⅔ Cup **Water**

ASSEMBLY

Beat the egg whites with the cream of tartar at slow speed until the mixture is foamy. Increase the speed to high until the whites are very stiff. Reduce the speed to low. Allow it to run while making syrup.

Dissolve the sugar in the water in a small, heavy bottomed saucepan. Once the sugar is completely dissolved, bring the heat to high until the syrup has reached 238° (soft ball stage).

Bring the mixer speed to medium. Pour the syrup in slowly. Bring the speed to high. Beat for 5 minutes, or until the bowl is cool.

Beat the cantaloupe puree into the mixture and freeze it in an ice cream freezer according to the manufacturer's instructions.

YIELD: 1½ quarts

FLOATING ISLAND PUDDING

6 *Eggs*
3 Tablespoons *Sugar*
4 Cups *Half and Half*
1 Tablespoon *Vanilla*
½ Cup *Sugar*

ASSEMBLY

Separate the eggs. Place the yolks in one medium-sized bowl and the whites in another.

Scald the half and half in a heavy bottomed saucepan over medium heat.

Whisk the egg yolks and the 3 tablespoons of sugar until the mixture is thick and light yellow.

Whisk in the scalded half and half. Strain the mixture back into the pan.

Cook over medium heat until the mixture coats the back of a spoon. Remove it from the heat. If the mixture begins to curdle while cooking, immediately pour it into a blender and blend on high speed until it becomes smooth.

Stir in the vanilla.

Cover and chill for at least 2 hours.

Whip the egg whites until they're stiff. Gradually beat in the ½ cup of sugar.

Fill a large frying pan three quarters full with water. Heat until just barely simmering.

Wet two tablespoons with water. Scoop up a heaping tablespoon of egg whites with one. Shape and push it into the shape of an egg with the other spoon. Place carefully into the simmering water.

Continue to shape and add "eggs" to the poaching water until you have about six in the water. Do not crowd them.

Cook each "egg" for 1½ minutes on each side. Drain each on a tray lined with paper toweling.

Cover and refrigerate the "eggs" or serve them right away with chilled sauce.

TO SERVE: Distribute the custard mixture equally into 8 individual dessert dishes or champagne glasses, then top each with the poached meringues.

SERVES: 8.

NOTES & TIPS

Use a copper bowl for beating the egg whites if you have one.

The French call these desserts *Oeufs a la Neige:* "snow eggs." The recipe is a basic one and can be enhanced in many ways: add sliced strawberries or fresh blueberries in the custard. Or shave chocolate over the "eggs." Top the whole dessert with a rosette of whipped cream and a mint leaf.

TARTE TATIN

8 *Golden Delicious Apples* peeled, cored, quartered
1½ Cups **Flour**
½ Cup **Butter** cut into 16 pieces
A Pinch **Salt**
¼ Cup **Cold Water**
¾ Cup **Sugar**
½ Cup **Butter**
¼ Cup **Sugar**

ASSEMBLY

Blend the flour, cut butter and salt in a food processor until the mixture is the consistency of fine crumbs.

Add the water. Process until the dough is just coming together.

Set on a smooth surface and knead about 5 times.

Wrap the dough in plastic wrap. Chill for 30 minutes.

Melt the butter in a 12 to 14-inch cast iron frying pan over low heat. Remove the pan from the heat.

Add the ¾ cup of sugar.

Place the apples round side down in a spiral pattern for first layer.

For the second layer place them cut side down in between the apples on the first layer.

Sprinkle the remaining ¼ cup of sugar over the apples.

Fold back any remaining pastry to make a lip.

Roll out the pastry into about a 16-inch circle. Cover the apples with the dough.

Bake at 425° for 45 minutes.

Turn it out while it's still hot by placing a pizza pan or baking sheet over the top of the frying pan and turning it quickly upside down. Be very careful while doing this because the pan is very hot and so is the syrupy mixture. It usually takes two sets of hands.

SERVES: 8

OVEN TEMP: 425°

Apples have more than just Biblical significance in the State of Washington. At a dinner in London in 1824, a young lady ate an apple, carefully wrapped the seeds and placed them in the vest pocket of a young man about to leave with the Hudson Bay Company for the Pacific Northwest. She asked that he plant the seeds when he arrived at his post. Other ladies thereupon put seeds of apples, pears, peaches, and grapes into the pockets of young men about to journey to the far west. From these seeds grew the first cultivated fruits in the Pacific Northwest.

CLASSIC APPLE PIE

1¾ Cup **Unbleached White Flour**
1 Pinch **Salt**
2 Ounces **Lard** cut into ½-inch pieces
4 Ounces **Butter** cut into ½-inch pieces
¼ Cup **Cold Water**
5 Cups **Apples** peeled, cored and sliced
¼ Cup **Sugar**
1 Dash **Nutmeg**
½ Teaspoon **Cinnamon**
3 Tablespoons **Flour**

ASSEMBLY

Place the flour and salt in the bowl of a food processor. Add the lard and butter.

Process this mixture until it is very fine, a little more course than corn meal.

Add the water and process until a ball of dough is just beginning to form.

Turn food processor bowl upside down onto a flour-covered surface and remove the dough.

Gently knead a couple of times to form the ball. Cut the ball in half; cover each half with plastic wrap. Chill for at least 30 minutes.

Place ½ of the dough on a flour-covered surface; gently roll it out using the following technique: roll the dough in one direction and turn after every roll to give an even crust and a uniform circle. If necessary, add a little flour to prevent it from sticking. Ease it into the bottom of a 10-inch pie plate; be sure it is not taut on the bottom.

Combine the remaining ingredients in a large bowl; mix well. Pour this mixture into the pie plate.

Roll out the remaining dough as above, place dough on top of pie, and crimp the edges. Cut off the excess dough.

Run your thumbnail around the edge of the pie plate to be sure the crust is not going to stick.

Cut 4 or 5 slits in the top to allow the steam to escape.

Bake for 10 minutes at 400°.

Reduce heat to 375° and bake for another 30 minutes.

SERVES: 6

OVEN TEMP: 400° & 375°

Klickitat County resisted government in its early days. After an 1860 election, no one took office because the citizens decided they didn't want other people running their lives.

PEACH MELBA CAKE

5 Ounces **Butter**
¾ Cup **Sugar**
3 Large **Eggs** beaten
¼ Teaspoon **Vanilla**
1 Cup **Self-rising Flour**
2 Cups **Raspberries**
½ Cup **Sugar** or to taste
4 Medium **Peaches**
¾ Cup **Apricot Jam**
1 Cup **Whipping Cream** whipped
8 **Mint leaves**

ASSEMBLY

Grease an 8-inch round cake pan. Set waxed paper, cut to fit, into the bottom. Grease the waxed paper. Coat the entire inner surface with flour, shaking out any excess.

Cream the butter with a wooden spoon or with an electric mixer, gradually adding the sugar. Continue to beat it until it reaches the consistency of whipped cream.

Beat in the eggs, a little at a time. Add the vanilla. Stir.

Fold in the flour. Turn it into a cake pan. Make a slight hollow in the center.

Bake for 30 minutes at 350°.

Remove it from the oven. Run a knife around the sides of the cake.

Flip it upside down onto a cooling rack lined with waxed paper. Lift the pan off carefully.

Place the raspberries in a strainer over a large bowl. Puree them by pressing them through the strainer with large spoon.

Add ½ cup of the sugar. Stir the mixture until the sugar has dissolved. Set the bowl aside.

Blanch the peaches. Peel and cut them into 12 slices each.

Heat the apricot jam over medium heat until it's melted. Stir thoroughly. Rub it through a strainer. Return it to the pan.

Split the cake in half. Place one half on a serving plate.

Reheat the glaze, adding water if it has become too thick.

Brush the glaze over the cut side of the cake.

Arrange half of the peach slices in a spiral over the glazed cake. Top them with the other half of the cake. Arrange the remaining peach slices on top; brush the glaze over the peaches.

TO SERVE: Cut the cake into 8 pieces. Pour a little of the raspberry sauce onto each plate and set a piece of the cake on top. Garnish with whipped cream and a mint leaf. Serve the remaining raspberry sauce in a small bowl with a ladle.

SERVES: 8

OVEN TEMP: 350°

IT'S ALL IN THE GRAPE

Washington wine varieties are named after distinct types of wine grapes, all of which have specific regional characteristics that set them apart from similar wines produced in other parts of the world. It was a surprise to many that certain areas of the state were capable of producing world class red wine grapes. The discovery was a welcome one, for today Washington Merlots, Cabernet Sauvignons, and Pinot Noirs have emerged on an equal footing with many of the finest of these wines produced worldwide.

Cabernets go well with roast beef, game and game birds, lamb, cheese, and fresh tuna. These wines should be served at cool room temperature.

Pinot Noirs are a good accompaniment to lamb, veal, beef, root vegetables, grilled snapper, salmon, halibut, sturgeon, chilled crab, and egg dishes. Serve cool (not refrigerated).

Washington Merlots use only the single Merlot grape, unlike French wines which traditionally mix Merlot and Cabernet grapes. The result is an elegant American wine that goes well with pate, beef, lamb, liver, cheese, vegetable mixtures, halibut, salmon—or just conversation. Serve cool (not refrigerated).

Adapted from *Vinyard to Vintage: The Washington State Wine Guide*. With permission of The Washington Wine Institute.

THE CHEF'S WINE SUGGESTIONS

Apple Cheddar Soup	*Chenin Blanc*
Carrot Peanut Soup	*Gewurztraminer*
Classic Apple Pie	*Ultra Late Harvest Riesling*
Cream of Broccoli Soup	*Gewurztraminer*
Gazpacho	*Sparkling Wine*
Peach Melba Cake	*Late Harvest Riesling*
David's Spinach Salad	*Sauvignon Blanc*
Spinach Soup	*Gewurztraminer*
Stuffed New Red Potatoes	*Pinot Noir*
Tarte Tatin	*Ultra Late Harvest Riesling*
Walla Walla Onion Soup	*Semillon*

EASTERN PLAINS

*E*migrants travelling to the Northwest found themselves dining on buffalo, sage hens, deer or antelope, and berries gathered along the way. Their introduction to the bounty of the area was inevitable since they had by that time probably run out of such staples as bread, bacon and coffee.

PATE MAISON

1 Pound Bulk **Italian Sausage**
1 Pound **Pork** ground
1 Pound **Veal** ground
1 Pound **Boneless, Skinless Chicken** ground
2 Tablespoons **Vegetable Oil**
2 Medium **Onions** chopped fine
½ Cup **Brandy**
3 **Eggs** beaten
2 Teaspoons **Soy Sauce**
½ Cup **Chopped Chives**
½ Teaspoon **Nutmeg**
½ Teaspoon **White Pepper**
1 Teaspoon **Garlic** minced
1 Pound **Bacon** sliced

ASSEMBLY

Brown the Italian sausage in a medium-sized frying pan. Drain off the fat. Set the pan aside to cool.

Combine the sausage with the pork, veal, and chicken in a large bowl. Set it aside.

Heat the oil in the frying pan (the same one used for browning the sausage) over medium heat.

Add the onions. Cook them until they're limp.

Add the brandy. Reduce it by half.

Pour this mixture over the meat.

Mix together: the eggs, soy sauce, chives, the nutmeg, white pepper, and the garlic. Pour this mixture over the meat.

Combine all of the ingredients thoroughly in the bowl.

Line two 2-quart loaf pans with bacon. Distribute the meat mixture and cover the pan with foil.

Place the pans in a bain-marie and bake at 350° for 2 hours.

Place a new piece of foil over the tops of the pans.

Place 2 more loaf pans on top of pates. Weight them down with heavy cans. Cool.

Refrigerate overnight.

TO SERVE: Remove the weights and unmold the pates. Slice them to the desired thickness and serve with melba toast or crackers.

SERVES: 2 loaves or about 50 slices.

OVEN TEMP: 350°

Kathryn Troxell, who travelled the Oregon Trail had this to say about early Northwest Cuisine: "Always the flavor of food depended on the fuel used—weeds, dry grass, sagebrush, or 'buffalo chips.;' "

WALLA WALLA ONION TYROPITAS

4 Cups **Walla Walla Onions** *chopped fine*
6 Tablespoons **Butter**
1 Cup **Swiss Cheese** *grated*
4 Ounces **Cream Cheese**
1 Dash **Nutmeg** *or to taste*
3 **Eggs** *beaten slightly*
½ Cup **Chives** *chopped*
¾ Cup **Unsalted Butter** *melted*
1 Package **Phyllo Dough**

ASSEMBLY

Melt the 6 tablespoons of butter in a medium sized saute pan over medium high heat. Add the Walla Walla Onions and stir to coat with butter.

Reduce the heat to low and cover the pan. Cook for five minutes.

Uncover the pan. Increase the heat to medium, cook until the onions turn golden brown, up to 40 minutes. Do not let the onions scorch. Remove the pan from the heat. Allow the onions to cool.

Mix well in a medium sized bowl: the Swiss cheese, cream cheese, and the nutmeg. Beat in the eggs. Fold in the chives.

Lay one sheet of Phyllo dough on a large cutting board with the long side of the dough toward you. Brush it with some of the melted butter. Lay another sheet on top. Brush it with butter. Repeat with one more sheet. Cut the Phyllo into seven strips lengthwise.

Place a scant teaspoon of the onion-cheese filling in the upper right hand corner of each strip. Fold the strip over to form a filled triangle. Fold over and over (like folding a flag) until there is a small filled triangle. Put each filled triangle (tyropita) on a baking sheet. Repeat until the filling is used up.

Brush them with melted butter. Bake at 350° for 25 minutes.

YIELD: About 70

OVEN TEMP: 350°

NOTES & TIPS

These can be prepared, except for baking, ahead of time. Simply set the cookie sheets with the tyropitas in the freezer for at least 30 minutes. Then you can put them into bags for freezer storage. To use them after they've been frozen, thaw them for about an hour before baking.

WALLA WALLA
ONION SOUP

6 **Walla Walla Sweet Onions** *peeled, sliced thin*
3 *Ounces* **Butter**
¼ *Cup* **Flour**
1¾ *Quarts* **Chicken Stock**
1 *Cup* **Johannisberg Riesling Wine**
¼ *Cup* **Dry Sherry** (Fino)
Freshly Ground Black Pepper *to taste*
1 *Cup grated* **Swiss Cheese**
2 *Tablespoons* **Parmesan Cheese** *grated*
8 **Dried French Bread Rounds** ½ *inch thick*

ASSEMBLY

Melt the butter in a heavy-bottomed 12 to 14-quart stockpot over medium high heat. Add the onions. Stir them well. Reduce the heat to low. Cover the pot. Cook for 30 minutes.

Uncover and cook until the onions are golden, stirring occasionally. (This may take up to 30 minutes or more .)

Sprinkle the flour over the onions. Continue cooking for 3 minutes. Remove from the heat.

Slowly stir in the chicken stock, wine, and sherry. Season with the pepper. Return the pot to medium high heat and stir until it boils. Reduce the heat to simmer. Cook for 8 minutes.

TO SERVE: Ladle the soup into ovenproof bowls and top each with a French bread round. Distribute the cheeses among the bowls. Place them in a 400° oven for 5 minutes or until nicely browned and bubbly.

SERVES: 8

If you do not have any ovenproof bowls, here is a system I have devised to use non oven-proof bowls. Place the French bread rounds on a baking sheet and distribute the cheeses over the bread. Place them under the broiler until the cheese is hot and bubbly. Place the rounds on top of very hot soup and serve.

Spokane House, the first permanent settlement in Washington, was established in 1810 by the North West company, a Canadian fur trading concern. It was located at the junction of the Spokane and Little Spokane rivers. The little post provided a resting place for fur traders and travellers as well as a trading post for the thousands of Indians who frequented the area.

CHICKEN VERONIQUE

10 **Chicken Breasts** boned, halved
2 Ounces **Butter** melted
1½ Cups **Chicken Stock**
1 Cup **Dry White Wine**
1 Cup **Cream**
3 Tablespoons **Arrowroot**
¼ Cup **Water**
1 Pound **Green Seedless Grapes** peeled

ASSEMBLY

Bake the chicken breasts on a baking sheet in a 350° oven for about 30 minutes or until they're done. Brush the chicken breasts with the melted butter after about 15 minutes.

Reduce the chicken stock and dry white wine by half in a medium saucepan over high heat. Add the cream. Bring it back to a boil.

Combine the arrowroot and water in a small bowl. Add it to the boiling sauce. Stir the mixture until it's thick.

TO SERVE: Just before serving, add the peeled grapes and heat through. Then using a slotted spoon, distribute the grapes over the chicken breasts and ladle the sauce over each breast.

SERVES: 10

OVEN TEMP: 350°

Chicken Veroniq

Yes, peeling the grapes is important: cooked grape skins are like cooked tomato skin. Unpleasant. And no, blanching doesn't work either. The dish is beautiful when finished; spending a little time ahead peeling grapes is definitely worth the trouble.

When reducing liquid, measure with a plastic ruler when you start to help you know when it's reduced by half.

CAPITOL CASHEW CHICKEN

*4 **Chicken Breasts** boned, split vertically*
*½ Cup **Cashews***
*1 Ounce **Butter***
*3 Tablespoons **Flour***
*1 Cup **Chicken Stock***
*3 Tablespoons **Cream***

ASSEMBLY

Bake the chicken breasts on a baking sheet at 375° for 35 minutes or until done.

Rinse the cashews in a strainer under running water to remove any salt. Bake them in a pie pan at 375° for 10 minutes.

Remove the cashews from the oven and allow them to cool. Chop them into small pieces.

Melt the butter in a medium sauce pan over medium heat. Add the flour. Cook for 2 minutes.

Remove from the heat. Stir the chicken stock in slowly.

Return to medium heat and stir until boiling. Allow it to boil for 3 minutes.

Stir in cream and cashews. Set aside.

TO SERVE: Heat 8 individual plates or one serving platter. Set cooked chicken breasts on the platter or individual plates, then coat each with a generous spoonful of sauce.

SERVES: 8

OVEN TEMP: 375°

The Governor's Mansion Foundation was organized in 1972 to furnish and decorate the public rooms of Washington's Executive Mansion in a "handsome and historically significant manner." The State is responsible for the building itself, but the non-profit foundation, begun through the efforts of Nancy Evans, then first Lady of the State, keeps up the public areas in the Mansion.

For the 1987 annual meeting of the Foundation, I developed this version of the more traditional cashew chicken. Since the Foundation is so helpful to those who work in the Mansion, I wanted something especially good for their get-together.

SPINACH STUFFED CHICKEN BREASTS

4 **Chicken Breasts** boned and split
1 Pound **Spinach** fresh, blanched, chopped
4 Ounces **Ricotta Cheese**
2 Tablespoons **Romano Cheese** grated
3 **Eggs**
2 Cups **Dry Bread Crumbs**
¼ Cup **Clarified Butter**
¼ Cup **Vegetable Oil**

ASSEMBLY

Cut a pocket lengthwise in the side of each breast ¾ of the way through using a small sharp knife.

Mix the spinach, cheeses, and 1 of the eggs thoroughly. Stuff 2 tablespoons of this mixture into each breast half.

Beat the remaining 2 eggs. Dip each breast half carefully into the eggs. Cover each with bread crumbs.

Set each aside on a baking sheet.

Heat the butter and oil in a 14–16 inch frying pan. Fry each breast for 15 minutes on each side.

SERVES: 8

NOTES & TIPS

To clarify butter, see p. 31

Maryhill Museum

James A. "Cashup" Davis, one of the most colorful pioneers in the Palouse, established a store and hotel on the Walla Walla-Colville stagecoach route. His nickname "Cashup" came from his habit, in this notoriously cash-poor area, of making his business offers always with the statement that he would pay a specified sum "cash up."

LAMB WITH TOMATOES AND GARLIC

20 **Lamb Loin Chops** 4 ounces each
50 Cloves **Garlic** peeled
1 Teaspoon **Dried Thyme**
¾ Cup **Unsalted Butter**
6 **Shallots** peeled and chopped fine
2 Cups **Cherry Tomatoes** halved
½ Cup **Dry White Wine**
½ Cup **Flour**
1 Teaspoon **Salt**
¼ Teaspoon **Black Pepper** freshly ground
½ Cup **Salad Oil**

ASSEMBLY

Cover the garlic and thyme in a medium-sized saucepan with water. Simmer for 30 minutes. Drain off the liquid reserving the garlic.

Melt ¼ cup of butter in a medium-sized frying pay over medium heat. Add the shallots. Saute until the shallots are limp.

Add the reserved garlic to the pan. Cook it until it's hot. Crush the garlic roughly with the back of a spoon.

Add the cherry tomatoes. Cook until the tomatoes are heated through.

Add the white wine. Reduce the liquid slightly.

Set it aside while cooking the chops.

Combine the flour, salt, and pepper in a shallow dish.

Heat 2 tablespoons of the oil over medium high heat in a frying pan at least 1½-inches deep.

Dip each chop in the flour mixture and brown each on both sides. Add the oil tablespoon by tablespoon as needed.

Place the browned chops on a baking sheet. Bake them at 350° for about 15 minutes for medium rare.

Return the sauce to medium high heat. Whisk in the remaining butter a tablespoon at a time.

TO SERVE: Place 2 chops on each plate. Pour a little of the sauce over each.

SERVES: 10

OVEN TEMP: 350°

Narcissa Whitman wrote from her house in Waiilatpu to her sister in New York in 1848, encouraging her to come west. "Bring as many girls as you can, but let every young man bring a wife, for he will want one after he gets here, if he never did before."

COUNTRY FRENCH PORK

3 Pounds **Boneless Pork Loin**
½ Pound **Bacon** sliced thin
1 Cup **Dry White Wine**
5 **Shallots** chopped fine
2 Pinches **Salt**
Freshly Ground Pepper to taste
¾ Cup **Cream**
2 Teaspoons **Dijon Mustard**
2 Tablespoons **Parsley/Chives** chopped

ASSEMBLY

Marinate the bacon, dry white wine, and shallots in a small bowl for 1 hour.

Roast the pork in a roasting pan at 350° for about 1 hour, until a meat thermometer registers 165°.

Remove and cover the pork.

Drain the marinated mixture; reserve the liquid. Fry the bacon and the shallots in a medium saute pan until the bacon begins to brown. Remove it from the heat and drain the excess grease.

Add the reserved liquid; reduce it by half over medium heat.

Add the cream; reduce it once again until it's thick.

Add the mustard. Stir it in well.

TO SERVE: Slice the pork into ½-inch slices; place them on a serving platter or heated dinner plates. Coat the meat with the sauce and garnish it with a bit of parsley or chives.

SERVES: 8

OVEN TEMP: 350°

I had been working at the Executive Mansion for only two weeks when I found that the French Ambassador was coming to dinner. I served this dish with Olympia oysters on the half shell, Salad Chinoise (See p. 84), and White Chocolate Mousse (See p. 168). It's not too difficult to imagine my anxiety serving a French dish for the French Ambassador, but it was a hit and I collapsed in relief.

At the lavish Davenport Hotel in Spokane, perhaps the greatest tourist attraction in the Inland Empire, washed coins were a speciality of the house. All change received at the Davenport was carefully washed and polished. It was said that "Davenport Dollars" were recognized as far away as New York and Washington, D.C.

PORK CHENIN BLANC

3 pound **Boneless Pork Loin**
2 Tablespoons **Oil**
¼ Cup **Brandy**
¼ Cup **Dried Apricots** chopped
¼ Cup **Dried Prunes** chopped
¼ Cup **Raisins**
½ Cup **Chenin Blanc**
2 Tablespoons **Butter**
2 Tablespoons **Flour**
½ Cup **Beef Broth**
¾ Cup **Half and Half**
1½ Tablespoons **Red Current Jelly**

ASSEMBLY

Heat the oil in a pan large enough to hold the pork. When it becomes very hot, brown the pork on all sides. Reduce the heat to low.

Heat the brandy. Pour it over pork. Ignite it to flame the roast.

When the flames have completely subsided, bake the pork for 45 minutes at 350° or when the pork reaches 165° on a meat thermometer.

Combine in a small bowl: the apricots, prunes, raisins, and wine. Marinate the mixture while the pork cooks.

When the pork is nearly done, melt the butter over medium heat. Add the flour. Stir well. Remove it from the heat.

Slowly stir in the beef broth. Return it to the heat. Bring it to a boil slowly, stirring it to prevent scorching.

Add the wine-fruit mixture, half and half, and the jelly. Bring it to a boil. Cook until it becomes thick.

When the pork is finished, cover it with foil. Allow it to rest for 10 minutes.

TO SERVE: Slice the pork into ¼-inch pieces and fan them out on individual heated plates or arrange them on a serving platter.

Pour the sauce over the pork just before serving.

SERVES: 8

OVEN TEMP: 350°

NOTES & TIPS

Serve a Washington State Chenin Blanc (of course) with Pork Chenin Blanc.

BRANDIED VEAL

2 Pounds **Boneless Veal Loin**
4 Ounces **Butter**
5 **Shallots** chopped fine
½ Cup **Brandy**
⅛ Teaspoon **Salt**
Freshly Ground Pepper to taste
2 Cups **Cream**
3 **Red Delicious Apples** cored, cut into ¼-inch slices
2 Ounces **Unsalted Butter**
A Light Sprinkling **Sugar** as needed

ASSEMBLY

Clarify the butter in a small saucepan by melting it over low heat. Skim off the residue that floats to the top. Spoon out the clear yellow liquid into a measuring cup, being careful not to disturb the milk solids that remain at the bottom of the pan. Set it aside.

Cut the veal loin into thin pieces and pound each between waxed paper.

Saute the veal, a little at a time, in a small amount of clarified butter in a saute pan over medium high heat.

Keep the veal warm on a baking sheet in the oven.

Saute the shallots in the remaining clarified butter until they're soft. Add the brandy, salt, pepper, and cream. Reduce the mixture until it coats the back of a spoon. Set it aside.

Melt the 2 ounces of butter in another saute pan over medium heat. Saute the apple slices gently until they are just starting to get translucent. Sprinkle them sparingly with sugar and cook until they start to carmelize.

TO SERVE: Arrange veal slices onto 8 warm dinner plates and top them with a spoonful of sauce. Garnish with 2 apple rings each.

SERVES: 8

NOTES & TIPS

A quick way to make the apple rings is by cutting the apples into ¼-inch slices then use a 1-inch round cookie cutter to take out the core.

Early fur trader Alexander Ross noted that, "At [the settlement of] Spokane House there were attractive buildings, a ball room even; and no females in the land so fair to look upon as the nymphs of Spokane; no damsels could dance so gracefully as they; none were so attractive."

VEAL FORESTIERE A LA CREME

8 **Veal escallops** 4 ounces each
½ Cup **Butter**
1 medium **Onion** chopped fine
½ Pound **Mushrooms** sliced thin
2 Tablespoons **Flour**
½ Cup **Chicken Stock**
¼ Cup **Dry Sherry**
2 Cups **Cream**

ASSEMBLY

Pound each escallop between 2 sheets of waxed paper.

Heat 2 tablespoons of the butter in a frying pan until it's foamy. Fry the escallops one at a time, adding more butter as needed. (Be sure not to overcook the veal.) Keep them warm on a platter in a low oven.

Set the pan over low heat. Add the remaining butter to the pan. Add the onions. Cook until the onions are soft.

Add the mushrooms. Cook for 3 minutes.

Remove the pan from the heat. Add the flour. Mix thoroughly.

Stir in the sherry and the stock. Return the pan to medium heat. Cook, stirring constantly, until the sauce boils.

Whisk in the cream. Reduce the mixture until it's thick enough to coat the veal.

TO SERVE: Heat 8 plates or a serving platter. Arrange slices of the veal on the platter or the heated plates. Coat them with the sauce.

SERVES: 8

SELAH
BARBECUE SAUCE

2 Tablespoons **Vegetable Oil**
¾ Cup **Chopped Onion**
½ Cup **Ketchup**
¼ Cup **Red Wine Vinegar**
¾ Cup **Frozen Apple Juice Concentrate** thawed
¼ Cup **Chili Sauce**
2 Tablespoons **Worcestershire Sauce**
2 Cloves **Garlic** minced
1 Teaspoon **Mild Chili Powder**
2 Teaspoons **Dry Mustard**

ASSEMBLY

Saute the onion in the oil in a medium sized saucepan and place it over medium high heat until it's soft, but not brown. Add the remaining ingredients. Cook the mixture until it reduces by half. Stir it occasionally to be sure the mixture does not stick to the pan.

YIELD: 1½ cups.

NOTES & TIPS

This sauce is a favorite of mine for barbecued spareribs. The apple juice concentrate makes an excellent tasty alternative to sugar or honey.

WILD RICE SUPREME

2 Cups **Wild Rice**
2 Quarts **Chicken Stock**
2 Ounces **Butter**
6 **Shallots** chopped fine
3 Stalks **Celery** chopped very fine
Orange Zest from 2 oranges
2 Ounces **Butter**
1 Cup **Walnuts** chopped fine
2 Tablespoons **Sugar**

ASSEMBLY

Wash and drain the rice thoroughly. Place it in a large saucepan along with the chicken stock. Bring it to a boil. Reduce the heat to low. Cook it covered until done, about 1 hour.

Melt 2 ounces of butter over medium heat and gently saute the shallots and celery.

Meanwhile place the orange zest in a small pan of cold water and bring it to a boil. Drain the zest, chop it, and add it to the butter-celery mexture.

Melt the remaining 2 ounces of butter in a medium frying pan over medium high heat. Add the walnuts. Reduce the heat to medium. Sprinkle the sugar over the top. Cook and stir the mixture until the sugar has carmelized. Be careful not to overcook. Remove it from the heat at once. Set the pan aside.

Mix the rice, prepared walnuts and celery mixture well in a large casserole dish. If the ingredients have cooled off, reheat in a 350° oven for 15 minutes.

SERVES: 8 with 1 cup servings.

NOTES & TIPS

A few years ago, I discovered the joys of a rice cooker; now I use it to cook all of my rice. As a matter of fact, I gave the Mansion one for Christmas in 1987 because the staff eats lots of rice for lunch. If you don't have a rice cooker, seriously consider buying one.

verfront Park and Spokane River

JULEKAKE: A HOLIDAY BREAD

½ Package **Quick Rise Yeast**
2 Teaspoons **Sugar**
¾ Cup **Hot Water** 110°
1 **Egg**
4 Cups **Unbleached White Flour**
1 Teaspoon **Ground Cardamom**
4 Ounces **Butter**
1 Cup **Golden Raisins**
½ Cup **Citron** chopped
8 Ounces **Almond Paste**

ASSEMBLY

Stir the yeast and sugar in the hot water until the yeast dissolves. Set it aside for 15 minutes.

Beat the egg into the yeast mixture.

Combine the flour with the ground cardamom. Cut the butter in with a pastry blender or food processor.

Place the mixture in a large bowl. Make a well in the center of flour. Stir in the liquid.

Place it on a floured board and knead it until it's smooth.

Knead in the golden raisins and chopped citron, a handful at a time.

Place the dough in a greased bowl. Turn it over once. Cover the bowl and set it in a warm place until it has doubled in bulk.

Work the almond paste by hand until it is pliable. Roll it out in the form of a long snake, about ¾-inch in diameter.

Roll the dough out into a long rectangle, about 5 inches wide. Lay the almond paste down the middle. Roll the dough up lengthwise.

Set the dough on a baking sheet with the seam side down. Allow it to rise for 45 more minutes.

Bake at 375° for 30 to 35 minutes.

Allow it to cool. Wrap in foil.

Set it aside for 24 hours to mellow in its wrapping.

SERVES: 12

OVEN TEMP: 375°

NOTES & TIPS

This can be frosted with a vanilla icing and sprinkled with sliced almonds if desired.

In an early cooking tip, The Emigrant's Guide to Oregon and Californis, 1845, warns that "good butter cannot be made on the road.... A can holding 6 to 20 quarts keeps our sour milk and cream, and makes our butter by motion of the wagon."

WHITE CHOCOLATE MOUSSE

6 Ounces **White Chocolate** chopped
⅓ Cup **Milk**
2 **Egg Whites**
1 Cup **Cream**
¼ Cup **Semi-sweet Chocolate Chips**
Strawberries as needed
½ Cup **Cream**

ASSEMBLY

Set the white chocolate in a small pan.

Scald the milk. Pour it over the white chocolate. Stir the mixture thoroughly over medium-low heat, until the chocolate melts. Remove the pan from the heat.

Allow the chocolate-milk mixture to cool.

Whip the egg whites until they're stiff. Fold them into the cooled white chocolate mixture.

Whip the 1 cup of cream until it's almost stiff. Fold it into the chocolate-egg white mixture.

Spoon the mousse into individual dessert dishes.

Cover. Chill them for at least 3 hours.

Melt the chocolate chips on an ovenproof plate placed on top of a pan of simmering water. Stir the chocolate with a teaspoon until it's smooth.

Dip each strawberry half way into the melted chocolate chips. Place them on waxed paper to harden.

Although Washington has had some gold in its hills, it's the gold in somebody else's hills that brought prosperity to Walla Walla. In the 1860s the mining activities in Idaho and Montana made that town a prosperous mercantile center.

Whip the half-cup of cream until it's stiff. Place it in a pastry bag fitted with a ¼-inch star tip.

TO SERVE: Pipe a rosette of cream on top of each mousse and place a strawberry on top of the cream.

SERVES: 6

Grand Coulee Dam

SLICED CHRISTMAS PUDDING

3 *Eggs*
¼ Cup **Apple Juice**
1 Tablespoon **Molasses**
1¼ Cups **Self-rising Flour**
2 Cups **Crumbs Fresh White Bread**
11 Ounces **Currants**
11 Ounces **Seedless Golden Raisins**
11 Ounces **Seedless Raisins**
¾ Cup **Beef Suet** chopped fine
½ Cup **Mixed Candied Peel** chopped
¼ Cup **Slivered Almonds**
1 Small **Apple** peeled, cored, grated
1 **Lemon** grated, rind and juice reserved
½ Teaspoon **Nutmeg** freshly ground
¼ Teaspoon **Allspice** ground
⅛ Teaspoon **Cloves** ground
1 Cup **Dark Brown Sugar**

ASSEMBLY

Beat thoroughly in a small bowl: the eggs, apple juice, and molasses. Set the mixture aside.

Set the mixer on low speed and add the remaining ingredients one at a time until they are thoroughly mixed and the flour is incorporated.

Mix in the liquid ingredients until the dry ingredients are moistened.

Distribute the mixture equally between two 2-quart greased loaf pans.

Cover the tops of each pudding with a rectangle of buttered parchment paper. Cover tops entirely with foil.

Pour water into the bottom of pans sufficiently large to hold a steamer rack. Place the steamer racks into the pans. Set the puddings on the racks. Steam for 5 hours, checking frequently to make sure the pans do not boil dry.

Remove the puddings. Cool them. Refrigerate.

TO SERVE: Slice thin pieces and arrange them on trays with a bowl of Fluffed Hard Sauce. (See Tips below.)

YIELD: 2 loaves or 40 slices.

NOTES & TIPS

An oriental stacking steamer works exceptionally well.

Fluffed Hard Sauce:
Cream ½ cup butter. Add gradually ½ cup powdered sugar. Beat in 3 tablespoons Calvados brandy, 1 tablespoon at a time. Refrigerate.

PASSION FRUIT ICE CREAM

16 **Passion Fruits**
4 Cups **Sugar**
4 Cups **Half and Half**

ASSEMBLY

Cut the passion fruits in half horizontally. Scoop out the seeds into a strainer set over a bowl.

Extract the juice from the seeds by rubbing them with the back of large spoon.

Add the sugar. Mix until it's dissolved.

Cover. Refrigerate for 2 hours. Freeze the mixture in an ice cream freezer according to the manufacturer's directions.

YIELD: 2 quarts

"Davenport waffles," served at the famed Davenport Hotel in Spokane, were an Eastern Washington taste treat over sixty years ago. Many people made the trip just for the waffles.

Goldendale

WHAT'S IN A NAME

Washington's distinct wine growing regions—the Yakima Valley, Walla Walla Valley, and the Columbia Valley (see map, page 178)—have been afforded official recognition as appellations. (*Appellation,* a French word, means *name.*) An appellation is like a pedigree, revealing the "true place or origin" of grapes in a wine. They tell the public what the vintners have always known: that the region where their grapes are grown is unique and different from any other region in the world. A wine labelled with an appellation signals the style, specific flavor characteristics, and aging qualities of the wine.

Interestingly, Washington's three official appellation regions are located in a semi-arid part of the state that experiences extremes of temperature. Fortunately, the Columbia, Snake and Yakima Rivers provide an abundant water supply, the soil drains well (an essential element), and the grape stock has been bred for winter hardiness. West of the Cascades, the longer, cooler growing season is ideal for German type wine grapes such as Müller-Thurgau, Madeleine Angevine and Riesling.

Adapted from *Vinyard to Vintage: The Washington State Wine Guide.* With permission of The Washington Wine Institute.

THE CHEF'S WINE SUGGESTIONS

Cashew Chicken	*Johannisberg Riesling*
Chicken Veronique	*Sauvignon Blanc, Semillon*
Country French Pork	*Pinot Noir*
Lamb with Tomatoes and Garlic	*Merlot*
Pork Chenin Blanc	*Chenin Blanc*
Sliced Christmas Pudding	*Late Harvest Riesling*
Spinach Stuffed Chicken Breast	*Gewurztraminer*
Veal Forestiere a la Creme	*Pinot Noir*
Brandied Veal	*Pinot Noir*

At "Cash Up" Davis' hotel near Steptoe Butte, local residents and travellers alike could enjoy a meal accompanied by music from a live orchestra— The Privett Brothers Stringed Orchestra. This even before the railroad arrived in Eastern Washington.

WASHINGTON WINES

*T*he first European grapes were
planted in Washington by German immigrants, west of Union Gap
and Yakima in 1871. Washington's
finest wine grape growing regions
share the same northerly latitude
as France's Burgundy and Bordeaux
regions.

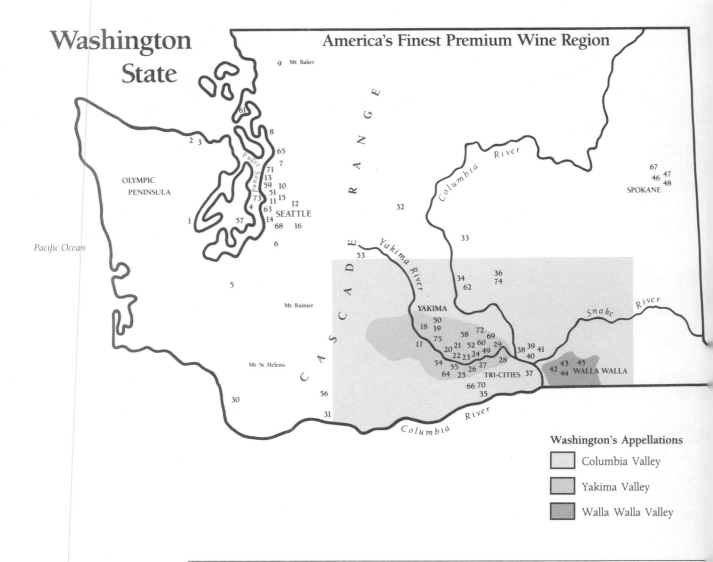

Washington State

America's Finest Premium Wine Region

9 Mt. Baker

OLYMPIC PENINSULA

Pacific Ocean

Puget Sound

61

8

2 3

65
7
71
13
59   10
51
73   15
4   11
63   12
14   SEATTLE
1   57   68   16
6

CASCADE RANGE

Columbia River

SPOKANE
67   47
46   48

32

33

53   Yakima River

34   36
62   74

Snake   River

YAKIMA
50
18   19
75   58   72
17   20   21   52   60   69
22   23   24   49   29   38   39   41
54   55   26   27   28   40
64   25   66   70   TRI-CITIES   37   42   43   45
35   44   WALLA WALLA

Mt. Rainier

Mt. St. Helens

30

56

31

Columbia   River

Washington's Appellations

☐ Columbia Valley

☐ Yakima Valley

☐ Walla Walla Valley

NUMERICAL LIST: WASHINGTON WINERIES

1 Hoodsport Winery
2 Neuharth Winery
3 Lost Mountain Winery
4 Bainbridge Island Winery
5 Johnson Creek Winery
6 Vierthaler Winery
7 Quilceda Creek Vintners
8 Pacific Crest Wine Cellars
9 Mount Baker Vineyards
10 Chateau Ste. Michelle
11 Columbia Winery
12 French Creek Winery
13 Haviland Vintners
14 E. B. Foote Winery
15 Paul Thomas Winery
16 Snoqualmie Winery
17 Staton Hills Winery
18 Covey Run Vintners
19 Horizon's Edge Winery
20 Stewart Vineyards
21 Tucker Cellars
22 Chateau Ste. Michelle
23 Yakima River Winery
24 Chinook Wines
25 Hinzerling Vineyards
26 Hogue Cellars
27 Pontin Del Roza
28 Blackwood Canyon Vintners
29 Kiona Vineyards
30 Salishan Vineyards
31 Mont Elise Vineyards
32 Wenatchee Valley Vintners
33 Champs de Brionne Winery
34 Langguth Winery
35 Columbia Crest Winery
36 Hunter Hill Vineyards
37 Caroway Vinyards
38 Quarry Lake
39 Bookwalter Winery
40 Preston Wine Cellars
41 Gordon Brothers Winery
42 Waterbrook Winery
43 L'Ecole No. 41
44 Woodward Canyon Winery
45 Leonetti Cellar
46 Arbor Crest Winery
47 Latah Creek Winery
48 Worden's Washington Winery
49 Barnard Griffin Winery
50 Bonair Winery
51 Cafe Juanita
52 Caroway Vineyards
53 Cascade Mountain Cellar
54 Cascade Cellars
55 Chamdanet
56 Charles Hooper Family Winery
57 Coolen Wine Cellars
58 Coventry Vale
59 Covey Run at Moss Bay
60 Donald Tocci Vineyard
61 Fidalgo Winery
62 Fox Estate
63 Horizon's Edge Winery
64 Hyatt Vineyards
65 McCrea Winery
66 Mercer Ranch Vineyards
67 Mountain Dome Winery
68 Newton & Newton Vintners
69 Oakwood Cellars
70 Redford Cellars
71 Salmon Bay Winery
72 Seth Ryan Winery
73 Staton Hills Winery
74 Tagaris Winery
75 Zillah Oakes

A BRIEF HISTORY OF WASHINGTON WINES

1871 The first documented planting of European vinifera grapes in Washington, planted by German immigrants in the Tampico area west of Union Gap and Yakima, in what is now the Yakima Valley Appellation.

1902 Irrigation was installed in the Sunnyside area which paved the way for future planting of grape vines.

1933 Prohibition was repealed in Washington State. The St. Charles Winery, the first to be bonded in the state, was opened on Stretch Island.

1934 Upland Winery, later named Santa Rosa Winery, opened in Sunnyside.

The Washington Liquor Control Act was passed by the legislature.

The Yakima Valley Grape Growers Association was formed.

1935 The Washington State Liquor Control Act was amended to permit "domestic wineries" using exclusively state grown fruit to sell wines direct to wholesalers and taverns. Wines from out-of-state could only be sold direct to the State Liquor Board.

1937 There were 42 bonded wineries in the state. Eighty percent of them failed before the advent of World War II.

1938 Vinifera and American grapes (labrusca) were planted at the Maryhill Museum along the Columbia Gorge.

Premium wine varietal grapes were imported from Europe then planted in Sunnyside.

Upland Winery was the first to blend vinifera grapes for their wines. A new Hungarian grape variety, Lemberger, was first imported.

1950 California threatened to boycott Washington apples if restrictive wine import measures were not removed.

1951 Premium grenache grapes were planted in the Yakima Valley.

1954 The American Wine Growers (AWG) was formed from a merger of two Washington wineries.

1960 There were eight active wineries in Washington.

1961 Associated Vintners (now Columbia Winery) incorporated.

Upland Winery was renamed Santa Rosa Winery and it released 14 different wines.

1965 Vineyard testing showed that the White Riesling was the most adaptable grape to the Washington climate. The AWG planted Riesling grapes near Grandview, Washington. These grapes later become the first premium wines released under the "Ste. Michelle Vineyards" label.

1967 The first release of wine under the Ste. Michelle label from American Wine Growers.

1969 On July 1 state laws were amended to permit "wine wholesalers." Competition from out-of-state wines revolutionized the wine business, causing all but three wineries to go out of business, and stimulating others to plant vineyards and plan premium wineries.

1971 Boordy Vineyards began producing Yakima Valley varietal wines in Prosser, Washington.

1972	The Wallace family established Hinzerling Vineyards near Prosser.
	The Sagemoor and Bacchus Vineyards, now suppliers to many Oregon and Washington wineries, were planted.
	The Mont Elise vineyards were planted near Bingen, on the Columbia River Gorge.
	The Kiona Winery vineyards were planted at the east end of the Yakima Valley.
1972-73	A severe winter caused extensive damage to Washington vinifera. A new technique for 'hardening of' vines was introduced, where they are gradually weaned off of irrigation water to prepare them for the winter.
	This technique protected vines during the severe winter of 1979.
1974	The AWG sold to Ste. Michelle Vintners Inc., which has become Washington's largest winery.
	Chateau Ste. Michelle's 1972 Johannisberg Riesling won the first national acclaim for a Washington wine.
	George Stewart, of Stewart vineyards, planted the first vinifera on Wahluke slope south east of Yakima, now a major grape growing area.

1976   Preston winery started by farmer Bill Preston, an inspiration to other farmer/vintners.

1978-79 Wahington vineyards experienced a major freeze which resulted in increased vinifera planting and winery development.

1979   Langguth became the first major European winery to invest in Washington.

1980   Worden's Washington Winery became the first in northeast Washington.

1982   The Yakima Valley was granted appellation status. The total wine grape acreage in Washington equalled 7,906 acres.

The Washington wine industry got a major boost when several important wineries opened. They included Hogue Cellars, Latah Creek, Mount Baker, Quail Run, Salishan Vineyards, Arbor Crest and Bainbridge Island Winery.

1983 The Walla Walla Valley was granted appellation status. The largest grape crop of wine grapes to date—21,300 tons—was produced.

1984 The Columbia Valley was granted appellation status.

There are now more than 50 bonded wineries in Washington State, and 11,000 acres planted with vinifera

Published with permission of The Washington Wine Institute.

CITY SANITARY SERVICE

GALLIVAN

"1982 — A VERY GOOD YEAR, EDDIE."

Robert Gallivan, Cartoonist

Robert Gallivan lives in southwest Washington. A graduate of the Chicago Academy of Fine Arts, his cartoons have appeared in the *Saturday Evening Post, Esquire, The New Yorker,* and other magazines. He served as an editor for the *Oregon Journal* in Portland.

Joel Levin, Photographer

Joel Levin works in commercial photography out of his downtown Seattle studio. His work takes him all around the state photographing everything from rodeos to the elegant dishes for the food photos in *Celebration*.

Nancy Pryor, Historian/Librarian

Nancy Pryor, who provided the historical vignettes for *Celebration*, is a native of eastern Washington, holding degrees from both Whitman College and the University of Washington. Recently retired as Northwest Librarian for the Washington State Library, she has spoken frequently on Northwest history, written a column on Northwest History for the *Pacific Northwest Quarterly* and published a number of bibliographies on Northwest writing.

Eric Wiegardt, Artist

Eric Wiegardt, who grew up on the Long Beach Peninsula in southwestern Washington and graduated from the University of Washington, studied art at the American Academy of Art in Chicago. He returned to Ocean Park, Washington, where he shows his watercolors at the Potrimpos Gallery. He has won prizes in the midwest and southwest and has work on display in galleries in New Mexico, Arizona, and Oklahoma. His watercolor, "Pike Place," appears in the cover art of *Celebration* and is reproduced completely on pages 12-13.

Mark Wiseman, Graphic Designer

Mark Wiseman has won awards for book design for *The Ark: Cuisine of the Pacific Northwest* and *Bay and Ocean*. His company, Wiseman Design in St. Louis, Missouri, holds both advertising and design awards from all over the country.

PHOTO CREDITS

Introduction

State Capitol   *Tom Stilz*

The Coastal Region

Crab Cioppino   *Joel Levin*
Salmon with Mustard
  Dill Sauce   *Joel Levin*
Salt Creek County Park   *Washington State Tourism Div.*
Seafood Fettuccine   *Joel Levin*
Ruby Beach   *Michael J. Salevouris*
Lemon Mousse
  with Blueberries   *Joel Levin*
North Head Light   *Washington State Tourism Div.*

Puget Sound

Ferry, Puget Sound   *Washington State Tourism Div.*
Vietnamese Stick Barbecue   *Joel Levin*
Eastern Washington Forest   *Michael J. Salevouris*
Seashell Pasta Salad   *Joel Levin*
Strawberry Blintzes   *Joel Levin*

Fertile Valleys

Stuffed New Red Potatoes   *Joel Levin*
Skagit Valley Tulip Field   *Tom Stilz*
Zillah Chili Soup   *Joel Levin*
Tulips   *Michael J. Salevouris*
Columbia River Gorge   *Tom Stilz*

Eastern Plains

Chicken Veronique   *Joel Levin*
Maryhill Museum   *Tom Stilz*
Riverfront Park   *Washington State Tourism Div.*
Grand Coulee Dam   *Washington State Tourism Div.*
Goldendale   *Washington State Tourism Div.*

INDEX OF RECIPES

(continued)

INDEX OF INGREDIENTS

(continued)

GALLIVAN